Gorbachev's Economic Strategy in the Third World

THE WASHINGTON PAPERS

. . . intended to meet the need for an authoritative, yet prompt, public appraisal of the major developments in world affairs.

President, CSIS: David M. Abshire

Series Editor: Walter Laqueur

Director of Publications: Nancy B. Eddy

Managing Editor: Donna R. Spitler

MANUSCRIPT SUBMISSION

The Washington Papers and Praeger Publishers welcome inquiries concerning manuscript submissions. Please include with your inquiry a curriculum vitae, synopsis, table of contents, and estimated manuscript length. Manuscripts must be between 120–200 double-spaced typed pages. All submissions will be peer reviewed. Submissions to *The Washington Papers* should be sent to *The Washington Papers*; The Center for Strategic and International Studies; 1800 K Street NW; Suite 400; Washington, DC 20006. Book proposals should be sent to Praeger Publishers; One Madison Avenue; New York NY 10010.

The Washington Papers/142

Gorbachev's Economic Strategy in the Third World

Giovanni Graziani

Foreword by Ernest H. Preeg

Published with The Center for
Strategic and International Studies
Washington, D.C.

PRAEGER

New York
Westport, Connecticut
London

Library of Congress Cataloging-in-Publication Data

Graziani, Giovanni.
    Gorbachev's economic strategy in the Third World / Giovanni
Graziani.
        p. cm. — (The Washington papers, ISSN 0278-937X : 142)
    "Published with the Center for Strategic and International
Studies, Washington, D. C."
    Includes bibliographical references.
    ISBN 0-275-93538-8 (alk. paper). — ISBN 0-275-93539-6 (pbk. :
alk. paper)
    1. Soviet Union — Foreign economic relations — Developing countries.
2. Developing countries — Foreign economic relations — Soviet Union.
3. Soviet Union — Commerce — Developing countries.   4. Developing
countries — Commerce — Soviet Union.   I. Title.   II. Series.
HF1558.15.D44G73   1990
337.470172'4 — dc20   89-71056

The *Washington Papers* are written under the auspices of The Center
for Strategic and International Studies (CSIS) and published
with CSIS by Praeger Publishers. The views expressed in these papers
are those of the authors and not necessarily those of the Center.

Library of Congress Catalog Card Number: 89-71056
ISBN: 0-275-93538-8 (cloth)
         0-275-93539-6 (paper)

First published in 1990

Praeger Publishers, One Madison Avenue, New York, NY 10010
A division of Greenwood Press, Inc.

Printed in the United States of America

∞

The paper used in this book complies with the Permanent
Paper Standard issued by the National Information Standards
Organization (Z39.48-1984).

10 9 8 7 6 5 4 3 2 1

Contents

Foreword   ix

About the Author   xiii

Acknowledgment   xv

Summary   xvii

1. The Economics of Soviet Policy in the
   Third World   1

   New Directions   1
   Soviet Reassessment of Third World Policy   3
   Changing Views of the Third World   7
   Development Models under Reappraisal   9
   Disagreements about the New International
        Economic Order   11
   Perestroika in the Domestic Economy and
        Foreign Trade   13

2. Soviet Economic Assistance to Developing
   Countries   16

   The Overall Value of Assistance   16
   Geographical Distribution of Aid   18
   The Debt Problem   22

v

The Quality of Economic Assistance   23
Renewed Emphasis on Efficiency   26

3. **The Geographical Orientation of Trade**   **30**

A Systems Approach to Trade Analysis   31
Trade Analysis by Economic Criteria   34
Trade by Regions and Individual Countries   37
A New Direction for Soviet Trade   40

4. **The Commodity Composition of Trade**   **43**

The Soviet Search for Food and Raw Materials   48
The Growing Importance of Fuels   52
Soviet Imports of Third World Manufactures:
    A Boom Ahead?   56
Soviet Machinery and Equipment: Breaking
    into the Southern Markets   60
Military Equipment Sales   68

5. **Trade Balances and Payments Arrangements**   **72**

The Trade Balance Triangle   72
Different Modes of Settlements   75
Countertrade   80

6. **New Forms of Economic Cooperation**   **83**

Turnkey Contracts   83
Production-Sharing and Buy-back
    Arrangements   84
Conversion Deals   85
Coproduction   86
Joint Ventures   86
Third Markets   91
Tripartite Industrial Cooperation   92

7. In Search of Strategy: Obstacles and Prospects   95

    No Room for Euphoria   96
    Soviet Interest in International Economic
       Organizations   98

Notes   101

Index   111

Foreword

Soviet economic relations with developing countries are not center stage in the evolving drama of Soviet President Mikhail Gorbachev's economic reform program, or *perestroika*. They do, however, play a significant role in Soviet trade prospects and, even more important, can have an impact on U.S.-Soviet relations in the Third World, where most East-West related violent conflict has taken place over the past 25 years.

Giovanni Graziani's book is a welcome development in piecing together this area of Soviet foreign economic relations. The relationship is ill-defined and notoriously lacking in up-to-date, hard information. Most data on Soviet economic aid abroad are classified state secret, and available trade figures are incomplete or, in some respects, inconsistent. Graziani does an admirable service in comprehensively assessing the available information and providing creative analysis of future prospects.

The point of departure is that Soviet economic strategy in the Third World derives from *perestroika* at home. Economic reform based on market prices, individual or enterprise-oriented incentives, an expanded private sector, and decreased emphasis on heavy industry has many parallels between internal Soviet reform and evolving Soviet economic relations with developing countries. I would summarize the change as fundamentally in the direction of the trade development strategy espoused by the United States, the World Bank, and Western donors.

The policy course for Soviet–Third World economic relations is still imprecise, however. As Graziani sums it up: "No coherent strategy has been officially announced or yet appeared in scientific journals. Rather, a new line is emerging from a series of random actions." Attitudes are still split on many issues, but more and more semiofficial thinking is with the reformers, which means a more market-oriented approach to relations with developing countries.

Moving from attitudes to realities brings out another parallel with internal *perestroika* — namely, the slow pace of actual change compared with statements of intent. Economic aid is still concentrated in Council on Mutual Economic Assistance partners — Cuba, Vietnam, and Mongolia. There is little evidence of new reform-oriented aid projects or a broadening of the share of aid disbursements to nonsocialist developing countries. In the trade field, Graziani estimates the Soviet exports of armaments to be on the rise, while the share for civilian manufactured goods may be declining to about 30 percent. The Soviet economic relationship with the newly industrializing countries is particularly elusive, and it is unclear whether it holds potential for Soviet export markets or, as appears more likely, a growing competitive threat. The most interesting and important relationship is with India, where the aid/trade relationship is most comprehensive, but even here the future course of economic relations is uncertain. Market-oriented economic reforms within both the Soviet Union and India may make traditional barter arrangements between the two countries less feasible while failing to produce commercially attractive alternatives.

There is thus a dynamic interplay between the incipient market-oriented internal Soviet reforms and the faster pace of such reform in many parts of the developing world. This can evolve in a mutually reinforcing way. Various "new forms" of economic cooperation are being tested, such as turnkey contracts, production-sharing arrangements, joint ventures, and tripartite industrial cooperation including a Western industrialized partner. The fact remains, however, that future Soviet export competitiveness in the Third World is very much in doubt. Developing countries are pressing the Soviet Union to import their manufactured products and not just basic foodstuffs and raw materials. But what will the Soviet Union export in return? Graziani explains that the touted Soviet overall trade surplus with developing countries may be largely a chimera. Dollar-denominated export prices in barter deals are often inflated, and long-term export credits tend to get rolled over or not paid at all. If Soviet military sales to the Middle East decline, as is likely, export accounts will be hit hard.

These are among the intriguing questions addressed in Graziani's book, and he provides the fullest treatment of them to date. But what are the implications for change in the Soviet relationship with developing countries on U.S.-Soviet relations, and what, if anything, should we do about them? This question goes beyond the scope of this volume, but there are clear opportunities at this stage for the United States to seek a more cooperative relationship with the Soviets in economic relations in the Third World.

In the area of economic aid, for example, cooperative efforts between the United States and the Soviet Union could help reduce tensions in some of the more troubled parts of the developing world. In October 1988, I visited Moscow to participate in a binational commission working group on economic aid to developing countries. The parallel thinking between internal economic reform and a revised approach to development in the Third World permeated our discussions. There was a clear understanding of the USSR's limited capability at this stage to make major changes in its aid and trade relations with developing countries. But there was also considerable interest among Soviet participants in working more closely with the United States and the international development institutions. A number of specific proposals for cooperative actions in the area of economic aid were developed and will be presented in a forthcoming book, jointly authored by Soviet and U.S. participants. Graziani's study provides the underlying analysis for what such initial cooperative steps might entail as well as the limitations they would face.

Ernest H. Preeg
The William M. Scholl Chair in
International Business
Center for Strategic and International Studies

About the Author

Giovanni Graziani is associate professor of international economics at the University of Brescia, Italy. Formerly he was associate professor of economics at the University of Padua. Professor Graziani has served as adviser to both the Italian government and the United Nations Conference on Trade and Development. His extensive writings on the USSR and on East European foreign trade and international economic relations include *Comecon, domination et dépendances* (Paris, 1982) and *Influence and Policy Implications of the Major Factors in Inter-Systems Trade, Especially East-South Trade* (Geneva, 1989).

Acknowledgment

Over the past two years, the Center for Strategic and International Studies has conducted a study of Soviet policy toward the Third World under Mikhail Gorbachev. The Soviet studies program of CSIS is pleased to acknowledge the generous support for this effort provided by the J. Howard Pew Freedom Trust.

Among the publications of this project are three Washington Papers, including the current work by Giovanni Graziani of the University of Brescia. The other two volumes are *Gorbachev's Military Policy in the Third World*, by Mark Katz of George Mason University, and *Gorbachev's "New Thinking" on Terrorism*, by Galia Golan of Hebrew University.

Stephen Sestanovich
Director of Soviet Studies
Center for Strategic
and International Studies
Washington, D.C.

Summary

Although Soviet economic relations with the Third World have generally been dictated by political, ideological, and military considerations, in recent years they have undergone fundamental reassessment and are now taking on an importance of their own. This volume contains Giovanni Graziani's interpretations of Mikhail Gorbachev's emerging new economic policy toward the Third World – an analysis backed by well-documented, sophisticated statistical analysis of Soviet economic assistance and trade. Graziani further substantiates his interpretations with a wealth of information from his interviews and research in the Soviet Union.

In chapter 1, Graziani enunciates Gorbachev's new, yet still incoherent, policy toward the Third World. Ineffective trade assistance to Third World countries is being reevaluated in light of domestic restructuring, which has necessitated cutting back on expenditures not related to internal purposes. The new economic relations with the Third World are characterized by (1) skepticism toward Soviet activism in the Third World as well as a criticism of the burden represented by aid to the Council for Mutual Economic Assistance developing countries; (2) avoidance of costly new commitments while commercial ties are being sought with such newly industrializing countries (NICs) as Brazil and South Korea; and (3) a growing reappraisal of the traditional development model based on state property, heavy industry, comprehensive planning, and import substitution.

Chapter 2 offers statistics on Soviet assistance to developing countries and the author's interpretation of this data. Graziani notes a distinct evolution of Soviet aid to the Third World under Gorbachev, with a notable increase in aid to the more developed and growing economies such as India, Brazil, and Egypt. Another new trend is the Soviet attempt to promote efficiency in the economies receiving aid.

Chapter 3 presents new insights on the changing Soviet attitude toward indebtedness and the growing dissatisfaction expressed by both the Third World and the USSR over the management of Soviet aid. The author's distinction between socialist and nonsocialist developing countries yields greater insight into the breakdown of Soviet export and import statistics and allows him to underline the accrued concentration of Soviet trade on the three CMEA countries and the minor importance of nonsocialist NICs. Although the author notes a contradiction between strategy and statistical evidence for Gorbachev's first years of leadership, he stresses that the recent moves to trade with South Korea and other Asian countries are bound to affect the Soviet geographical pattern of trade.

The author's statistics in chapter 4 show new developments in the composition of Soviet trade with the Third World. The author documents the increasing importance of agricultural products and fuels in Soviet imports and of military equipment and fuels in exports. The use of fuel for both export and import is described by the author as the "oil imbroglio." To stabilize its export earnings in hard currencies threatened by falling oil prices, the USSR has increased its imports of crude oil from the Third World for reexport to the West.

The author shows that the Third World requests for a larger share of manufactures in its exports to the USSR are well grounded, because the USSR's share stands at a much lower level than the West's. There is a rationale for the Soviets to expand manufactures imports from the Third World because the sector is internally underdeveloped and plagued by labor shortage. On the other hand, the author challenges the traditional view of Soviet success in manufactures exports to the Third World and forecasts gloomy short- and medium-term prospects. Low technical standards in quality and finishing, as well as the lack of spare parts and after-sales service of Soviet manufactures, are documented from both Third World and Soviet literature. Harsher competition from the Third World, especially from the NICs, even in success-story sectors such as chemicals and cars, is well evidenced by an approach in terms of market shares.

In chapter 5, Graziani criticizes the assumption that the Soviet surplus in convertible currencies with the South tends to compensate deficits with the West. Most Soviet trade with the Third World is conducted through complex barter or clearing agreements, and the USSR generally incurs deficits in its convertible currency trade with the Third World and achieves surpluses from the export of military equipment and strategic materials. The author also details the use of countertrade agreements between the USSR and developing countries. These agreements are not necessarily efficient, but have the advantage of reducing convertible currency expenditures. Thus he predicts they may continue as the main form of trade for the Third World.

Chapter 6 contains an original analysis of the numerous other new forms of economic cooperation being used to expand trade with developing countries. Graziani pinpoints and discusses turnkey contracts, buy-back and conversion deals, joint ventures, and tripartite industrial cooperation, using a wealth of examples and statistical material. The author suggests that these new forms may in the future constitute the backbone of mutual trade.

Perestroika has led to a reassessment of Soviet commitments in the Third World, which will probably lead to an increase in trade with the more profitable, developed Third World markets and a subsequent reduction of trade with the less developed economies. Eventual Soviet participation in international economic organizations could entail further conflicts with the Third World. Until Gorbachev's economic policy towards developing countries becomes more consistent and coherent, however, predictions about the Soviet–Third World economic relationship must be seen as educated conjecture.

1

The Economics of Soviet Policy in the Third World

New Directions

Mikhail Gorbachev has distinguished himself from his predecessors by his willingness to confront a long-avoided issue – the dismal economic performance of the Soviet Union, which thwarts the USSR's efforts to become a full-fledged superpower. According to Ivan Ivanov, deputy chairman of the powerful State Foreign Economic Commission, "the Soviet Union should firmly occupy a place on the world market according to its scientific and technological potential and political weight" – a place it obviously does not occupy today.[1]

Understandably then, internal economic reform has the highest priority on Gorbachev's agenda. Most Soviet resources are currently needed for internal purposes, and the rest must be thriftily used according to the strictest priorities. Military expenses, which weigh too heavily on the budget, must be reduced, requiring détente to be encouraged and international tensions defused. Although Soviet foreign policy surely cannot be reduced solely to an economic dimension, on the whole economics seems to be a more solid issue than it was.

Meanwhile, the entire Soviet perception of world rela-

1

tions has changed. More in line with today's realities, the present Soviet concept stresses the globality of problems and a growing tendency toward interdependence among different economies and states. Sanctioning a line of thought already elaborated by various analysts in the latter 1970s, Gorbachev's report to the 27th Congress of the Communist Party of the Soviet Union (CPSU) in March 1986 states that "a contradictory but interdependent and, in many respects, integral world is taking shape."[2] The Stalinist Manichaean thesis of "two camps" (the capitalist and the socialist) irreconcilably opposed to each other is officially buried. One single world market dominates. Universal problems affect both capitalist and socialist states and constitute the basis for effective cooperation.

This integral concept of interdependence, together with Gorbachev's economic priorities, has three main implications for his foreign policy. They call for (1) a multipolar approach in Soviet diplomacy (instead of a traditionally unidirectional one), (2) a military build-down, and (3) a defusion of regional conflicts.

In all three spheres, actual behavior has supported the announced theoretical positions and illustrated the new global approach. In the diplomatic arena, the Soviets have continuously searched for agreements with the United States. They have fostered official mutual recognition between the European Community (EC) and the Council for Mutual Economic Assistance (CMEA), which took place in June 1988; sought to adhere to the General Agreement on Tariffs and Trade (GATT) and a changed attitude toward the International Monetary Fund (IMF); and, finally, inaugurated the new Asian diplomacy. Gorbachev speaks of Asia as a "common house from the Pacific to the Urals." He favors concessions to China and Japan to solve long-standing border problems and attempts new commercial ties with South Korea and Asian countries, while launching a diplomatic offensive toward moderate, large, and relatively wealthy developing countries in Latin America and the Middle East.

Gorbachev's initiatives in the area of disarmament are well known and will not be discussed in detail here. Aside from the announced unilateral reduction of Soviet armaments, it is enough to recall the agreement reached in Paris in January 1989 on halting and destroying chemical weapons. This event is politically significant to our subject because the Soviet Union has aligned itself more with the positions of the advanced capitalist countries than with those of many developing countries that want to tie the issue of chemical weapons to nuclear disarmament.

As for the defusing of regional conflicts, some Western analysts have been cautious in recognizing actual deeds by the present Soviet leadership.[3] But, more examples exist to support a policy of defusion than to negate it. China has welcomed the unilateral reduction of Soviet military forces (which will affect mostly Mongolia and the borders with China) as a "positive development" in mutual relations. The USSR's decision to withdraw troops from Afghanistan had a more resounding impact, as did the pressures the USSR put on two of its closest, most heavily subsidized clients in the Third World (Vietnam and Cuba) to withdraw their troops from Kampuchea and from Angola respectively. Even the case of Libya reveals Soviet cautiousness and a low propensity for taking risks. Gorbachev exercised the prerogative of a global power acting in its own interests when deciding to install Sam-5 missiles in late 1986 and to sell six Sukhoi-24D fighter-bombers early in 1989. Yet he refused to sign with the unreliable Libya a treaty of friendship and cooperation that would include military assistance in case of war. Soviet reactions to the two U.S. raids in 1987 and to the shooting down of two Libyan MiGs in January 1989 were verbally strong, but militarily rather mild.

Soviet Reassessment of Third World Policy

How do the developing countries fit into this new picture? A general reassessment of Soviet Third World policy has been taking place under Gorbachev.[4] No coherent strategy has been officially announced or yet appeared in scientific journals. Rather, a new line is emerging from a series of random actions, declarations of intent, and laws affecting the economic sphere. The new line still needs to be articulated as a proper overall strategy. The apparatus (party bureaucracy) and scientific community are still divided between defenders and supporters of this new course; many take an intermediate position. Some scholars still see the Third World through the political-ideological prism of "imperialism" or "socialism." Many foreign trade officials still have bureaucratic methods of managing foreign economic relations. On the whole, however, it is safe to say that attitudes and initiatives are undergoing a profound reappraisal.

The time when the USSR expressed all-out support for national liberation struggles seems to be gone. At best the CPSU program presented to the 27th Party Congress extends "profound sympathy for the aspirations of peoples who have experienced the heavy and demanding yoke of colonial servitude."[5] In his address to the same congress, Gorbachev does not even consider the Third World in a separate discussion.

Is the Third World losing importance in the eyes of the Soviet leadership? The declared Soviet intention to concentrate on domestic economic problems through reforms and the restructuring of the foreign trade system — in particular, the new legislation on joint ventures in the USSR, apparently tailored for relations with the industrialized West — might suggest such an impression. Yet this new attitude should be taken more as a sign of dissatisfaction with the current state of affairs than as a determination to reduce these ties.

The skepticism about Soviet activism that characterized the latter part of Leonid Brezhnev's time in office (first in Angola and Mozambique, later in Ethiopia, and finally in Afghanistan) was already mounting in the late 1970s in the scholarly community. Many of these adventures were increasingly seen as Pyrrhic victories; in an attempt to sustain some of the poorest countries in the world, they drained a Soviet economy already plagued by declining growth rates. The burden represented by the massive economic aid extended to some developing countries co-opted in the CMEA was meeting with growing criticism among the more developed partners. The refusal to admit Mozambique and Laos into the CMEA seems to reflect the same mood.[6]

The CPSU program both echoes and sanctions this new attitude by asserting that the "socialist-oriented" developing countries should advance "mainly through their own efforts," with the USSR assisting them in the future "to the extent of its abilities."

The phrase "socialist-oriented" (or "countries with socialist orientation") gained considerable currency in the late 1960s. Replacing the old expression "noncapitalist path," it came to denote those developing countries that had firmly committed themselves to socialist principles and were characterized by a Marxist-Leninist vanguard party, a large state sector, and the nationalization of foreign capital. Although no full agreement has ever existed in the literature or in official statements on the number of nations in this category, the general tendency today is to include the four countries mentioned above—Angola, Mozambique, Ethiopia, and Afghanistan—plus South Yemen. More recently, Nicaragua could also be added. All of these countries enjoy observer status at the CMEA. Official Soviet documents consider Mongolia, Cuba, and Vietnam (members of the CMEA) to be full-fledged socialist states, as well as China, North Korea, Yugoslavia, and sometimes Laos and Kampuchea.

A thorough reevaluation of the experience of socialist-oriented countries had already begun in the latter 1970s, culminating in a 1982 book that challenged all previous certitudes.[7] According to this volume, these states are still considered progressive, but are believed to be presocialist, because social conditions do not allow full socialism. In fact, they could even revert to the old capitalist path. As a consequence of global interdependence, these countries not only have failed to sever their ties with the world capitalist system, but should make every effort to integrate even further into it by allowing inter alia Western foreign investment and assistance. An acceptance of private capital and a parallel reduction of the role of the state are also advocated. Finally, the so-called vanguard parties are seen as incompletely formed proletarian parties, because of the incomplete process of class formation: indeed, these countries should push for the formation of united fronts instead of Marxist-Leninist parties.

Like the West, the USSR has a political approach to economics in its relations with the Third World. In the past 30 years, however, political and ideological considerations have loomed much larger in shaping Soviet economic relations with the developing countries than in shaping Western economic relations with these countries. Secondary as it may have been when Nikita Khrushchev launched the first offensive toward the Third World, the economic dimension has gradually gained importance for Soviet decision makers after Brezhnev's accession to power.

Especially in the later years of his leadership, Brezhnev applied a dual policy toward the Third World: all-out political-military support for progressive regimes went hand in hand with a more pragmatic orientation in economic ties.[8] Neither does Gorbachev throw out the baby with the bath water. While keeping the old clients, he has tried to avoid costly new commitments in remote, high-risk areas and has emphasized the need to depoliticize most issues related to the Third World and to restructure overall economic relations "within" the Third World to make benefits genuinely "mutual."[9]

The new openings toward "the young states which are travelling the capitalist road" and with which "real grounds of co-operation" exist should be read within this framework.[10] Since 1986, Gorbachev has paid two visits to India to consolidate ties with the USSR's most important commercial partner in the nonsocialist developing world. Soviet Foreign Minister Eduard Shevardnadze visited Mexico (in October 1986) and Brazil, Argentina, and Uruguay (in September 1987). Diplomatic relations were established in 1985 with Oman and the United Arab Emirates (UAE). Normal diplomatic relations are expected with Saudi Arabia, now that Soviet withdrawal from Afghanistan has been completed, and the USSR has tried to maintain good relations with Iran. Finally, there has been an upswing in bilateral visits with such Asian countries as Malaysia, Indonesia, Thailand, and the Philippines, while the first commercial ties have been established with South Korea and discreetly hinted at with Taiwan.

Reinforcing relations with these countries has the fundamental rationale of deepening economic ties with nations more developed and in most cases more solvent than the friendly socialist-oriented countries. Soviet analysts go to great pains to find political justification as well. According to some, a fruitful political cooperation can be reached with both the countries that uphold "national sovereignty" in their policies toward Western "imperialism" and those largely "dependent on Western imperialist powers" but having "influential forces within the ruling circles . . . [that] orient themselves to national interests."[11] Still, economic motivations seem to prevail.

Changing Views of the Third World

Such a broad reappraisal of Soviet policy toward the Third World also results from new perceptions about the Third World itself, articulated at first during the 1970s and further developed in the 1980s. The Khrushchev era emphasized the unity of the Third World and the USSR as the natural ally of Third World countries. These views began to lose ground during the late 1960s and the early 1970s. Instead of unity, the growing diversification among developing countries was acknowledged. By 1976 a book appeared containing the first socioeconomic typology of the developing countries.[12] The same 31 indicators were applied to 85 nations, divided into four basic categories. This approach was further refined in the 1980s, especially at the Institute of World Economy and International Relations (IMEMO). Two of the institute's leading researchers published, in two successive books, the most authoritative position on the subject.[13] In their 1987 book, authors Anatoly Elyanov and Victor Sheinis use an integrated approach incorporating several socioeconomic features (gross domestic product, or GDP, per capita, size of population, territory, natural resources, development of modern sectors, scale of precapitalist structures, etc.) to analyze 140 countries for the period 1950–1980. As a result, they establish seven major groups of developing countries arranged in four levels. The upper echelon, characterized by a relatively high per capita income, encompasses three groups of countries: (1) the more advanced countries in Latin America and the small states in both the Far and Middle East, who share cultural and historical development with the European peoples; (2) the oil-exporting countries, and (3) other small states and territories with a high per capita income.

The upper-middle echelon includes only one group of countries (4), whose per capita income is slightly higher than the average, but where preindustrial forms of labor still dominate the economy. The lower-middle echelon (5) embraces countries whose per capita income is well below the average and whose domestic market and differentiated structure are poorly developed. Within the lower echelon, a special group (6) is singled out that includes three highly populated countries with low per capita incomes – India, Indonesia, and Pakistan. Last are (7) the countries very similar to the United Nations (UN) grouping of least-developed countries. Here the per capita income is so low and grows at such a slow rate that it often falls short of the survival minimum for a greater part of the population.

Although some rankings are curious (Taiwan and South Korea are included only in the fourth group, and not in the first), it is interesting to note that the "socialist-oriented countries" belong either to the fifth or to the seventh group, at the bottom of the scale. For some, such as Ethiopia, it is openly said that "the economic situation is very difficult and, at times, catastrophical."[14] In line with an apolitical approach, the Socialist-oriented countries are not treated in a separate chapter or even paragraph, but only slightly touched upon here and there.

Even more sweeping is the departure from past ideologized conceptions of the Third World. As the same authors state bluntly, not only has there never been a real unity among the developing countries, but also the gap between the economic development levels is growing. The authors do not indicate the countries toward which the Soviet Union should reorient most of its foreign economic activity. Recent initiatives reveal a marked preference for the upper echelons, however.

Development Models under Reappraisal

The development model applied to the Third World is nowadays under increasing criticism. Under Khrushchev the model duplicated Soviet historical experience: sweeping nationalization, a large state sector, high rates of accumulation, big projects in heavy industry, import substitution, comprehensive planning, looser ties with the capitalist countries, and closer ties with world socialism. Failures of this model both in the USSR and in some of the developing countries that tried to apply it pushed some specialists to begin to reappraise it under Brezhnev.[15]

Under Gorbachev, revision seems to be legitimate, although more orthodox positions still remain. A simultaneous and interrelated growth of accumulation and consumption in various sectors of the economy is now advocated.

Instead of the previous preference for heavy industry, new models are based on a more balanced growth between agriculture and industry (especially light industry), with agriculture receiving special privilege. Small and medium-sized enterprises are now recommended instead of large facilities. Specialization on natural resources and the resulting commodities is no longer disdained; to the contrary, it is even seen sometimes as a way to obtain foreign currency necessary to import the basic industrial equipment needed to spur industrialization. Developing countries are encouraged to process more of their primary commodities so as to take better advantage of cheap local labor.

At the same time these countries find it expedient to try to accelerate the development of high-technology industries and create a modern, export-oriented sector. Whatever the privileged sector, the most striking element of all these proposals is the emphasis on export-led growth, instead of the earlier import substitution model based on protection. The Southeast Asian development model and the reasons for its success, together with the failure of the Latin American model, are closely scrutinized in the most important research institutes. There is also a new favorable attitude toward the private sector. Ideological justification is, at times, found in the New Economic Policy (NEP) period of the Soviet Union. The state sector, once considered the key to development, is now increasingly criticized for being inefficient, for destructive interference in the economy, and for corrupting the ruling classes. The role of foreign capital and transnationals is regarded less negatively; the USSR itself tries to attract foreign capital. Moreover, neither cooperation between developing countries themselves nor between them and the socialist countries is considered an alternative to the promotion of economic ties with the industrially advanced states. Even anti-imperialism is no longer considered to be a criterion of social progress: the experience of fundamentalist Iran, the Kampuchea of the Khmer Rouge, and Idi Amin's Uganda are sometimes quoted as examples of new forms of exploitation and social regress.[16]

Disagreements about the
New International Economic Order

The Khrushchevian myth that the Third World is a natural ally of the socialist countries has also been harshly criticized in the past decade; this criticism is particularly noticeable in the USSR's position on the New International Economic Order (NIEO) — that is, new codes of international conduct to protect developing countries.[17] Here the mid-1970s also was a watershed. At the fourth UN Conference on Trade and Development (UNCTAD) held in Nairobi in May 1976, the developing countries presented for the first time the same set of demands to the socialist countries as to the industrialized West. Five months later the first Soviet criticisms of that platform appeared. In a declaration submitted to the UN General Assembly, together with a general support for Third World positions, the USSR stated that

• the Soviet Union cannot be held responsible for the colonial past and thus should not be asked to devote a certain percentage of its GNP to assist developing countries;
• the Soviet Union is opposed to all kinds of protectionism and discriminatory practices, not just those affecting the Third World; and
• the increase of aid should be looked at within the framework of disarmament, which the platform fails to do.[18]

At the fifth UNCTAD session in Manila (1979), it elaborated on the same theme. According to the USSR, the NIEO should include a restructuring of all sectors of world trade, not only those affecting the Third World, and international economic relations can be made more democratic even before the elimination of capitalism.[19]

Many criticisms also started appearing in the writings of specialists about Third World demands for preferential treatment,[20] about the whole program presented by the de-

veloping countries (considered too utopian and distribu-
tion-oriented),[21] and about the concept of collective self-reli-
ance (its extreme interpretation would mean economic sepa-
ratism).[22] In short, the Soviet position points out that the
program of the NIEO proceeds from the assumption that
only the Third World is interested in changing international
economic relations, while such restructuring is a global
problem that requires a global approach. The need for new
approaches toward international economic and political
relations is stressed, with the concept of "international
economic security" being the expression of such new
approaches.[23]

The claims of the Third World have been repeated at
practically every UNCTAD session. The more specific demands advanced by the developing countries at the seventh
UNCTAD session (1987) held in Geneva and at various other international meetings might be synthesized in the following list:[24]

• greater economic assistance from the socialist countries and better conditions in the granting of credits
• an increased share of convertible currencies in the
financial resources destined to finance projects in the Third
World
• attention to the specific needs of the least-developed
countries
• creation of a more flexible and efficient mechanism
for international settlements (payments)
• a larger share of manufactured and semi-manufac-
tured products in developing countries' exports
• preferential treatment as an integral part of the principles of international trade and not as an exception (as the
Soviet Union would like)[25]
• finally, a clearer identification of the most promising
export groups for the developing countries.

These points represent some of the chief unresolved
problems in Soviet–Third World relations.

Perestroika in the Domestic Economy and Foreign Trade

The different aspects of Soviet–Third World economic relations should be analyzed within the framework of the broad restructuring (*perestroika*) of the domestic economy and of foreign trade now under way in the USSR. The fundamental objective appears to be the elimination of inefficiencies in the so-called extensive model of development, which is based upon continuously adding productive factors instead of enhancing productivity (intensive model). To this end, more play is given to market mechanisms, while many mandatory indicators formerly imposed on enterprises are being reduced. Productive units are now urged to operate on a self-financing basis, without state subsidies. Other changes include the possible liquidation of enterprises, their horizontal linking, stricter state control on the quality of industrial products, and the enlargement of the individual and cooperative sector.

Far more important for our purpose is the thorough reorganization of the foreign trade system. The first aspect of reorganization is the right granted to enterprises, organizations, ministries, and republics to have direct relations with foreign partners, without having to pass through the filter of a central body. By December 1988, 140 such entities had acquired this right, covering 22 percent of Soviet exports and 32 percent of its imports, mainly in the manufacturing sector. On April 1, 1989, this right was extended to all enterprises and cooperatives, provided that they produce competitive goods. Most important, they can retain a share of the hard currency receipts obtained from exports.

The Ministry of Foreign Economic Relations (created in January 1988 by the merger of the former Ministry of Foreign Trade and the State Committee of Foreign Economic Relations) still holds under its direction, however, 25 foreign trade organizations responsible for the export of fuels and raw materials and for the import of foodstuffs and other commodities. In the longer term, two acute problems will be tackled: one is the connection between world and domestic prices, which today is very loose and does not allow for a precise calculation of export/import profitability; the second, closely related problem has to do with gradual progress toward convertibility and toward an exchange rate more realistic than the present, artificial one.

In this context, three momentous decisions made in December 1988 are worth noting. The first is the commitment, on January 1, 1990, to devalue the ruble by 100 percent for export-import transactions of Soviet enterprises in hard currencies; the second is the decision to establish a state-controlled auction for foreign currencies among Soviet enterprises to test the market rate of the ruble; and the third, beginning a year later, is to stop using some 3,000 "differentiated currency coefficients" currently sheltering the domestic price structure from world prices in favor of a single exchange rate. These coefficients were introduced in early 1987 to bridge the gap between domestic and international prices, to raise the effectiveness of Soviet exports, and to reduce irrational imports, but they have resulted in an unwieldy and cumbersome system widely criticized in the Soviet press.

A new model of foreign economic relations is now advocated, based on a completely different structure of Soviet exports. The present accent on energy products exposes Soviet revenues to the vagaries of international prices for energy and raw materials. As a result, more value-added products should be represented in the Soviet export mix.

The second aspect of reorganization is the 1987 laws allowing, for the first time, joint ventures on Soviet territory and renewed Soviet foreign investment abroad. Obtaining more hard currencies from exports, acquiring high technology goods, and substituting irrational imports are official motivations for joint ventures. Special economic zones for joint ventures are foreseen at the Finnish border, in the Soviet Far East and Siberia, with particularly favorable customs and licensing regimes and lower prices for natural resources and labor.

The final aspect of reorganization is a much broader issue. The USSR wants to integrate its economy progressively into the international division of labor and participate in the work of international organizations. The official recognition of the EC was a step in this direction; the semi-official contacts with the Bank for International Settlements, the new openings on the IMF, the World Bank, and the GATT appear to be proceeding along the same path.

2

Soviet Economic Assistance to Developing Countries

The Soviet Union does not distinguish between the transfer of resources and purely commercial transactions, but includes both under the all-embracing concept of economic cooperation. Aid and trade are also closely connected in Soviet practice, because most of the aid consists of deliveries of goods and services, and repayments are made in the same way. As a result, it becomes all the more difficult to evaluate the exact amount of Soviet assistance.

The Overall Value of Assistance

Until 1982 the USSR did not release data on the overall volume of Soviet economic assistance, let alone its geographical distribution. Since then, a series of official declarations have begun to reveal the overall amount and its relation to the Soviet gross national product (GNP), plus some of the conditions attached to the assistance. In the latest of these documents, the USSR claims that in 1987 the net volume of Soviet credit and financial assistance to the Third World amounted to ruble (R) 11.7 billion (U.S. $18.5 billion), which is equivalent to 1.8 percent of Soviet GNP.[1] With this figure the USSR would be well ahead of any other nation in the world on the list of donors and would more than satisfy the UN's targeted ratio of 1 percent aid to GNP.

On the contrary, Western estimates are about four-and-a-half times lower than these claims, with the gap increasing over time. The reason is rather simple. The USSR uses in its calculations many items that are not included in the conventional Western definition of official development assistance (ODA) – that is, official grants and loans characterized by a grant element of at least 25 percent. To these calculations the USSR adds the following: the impact of preferential prices in trade – that is, price subsidies paid for Cuban sugar and nickel and for Mongolian raw materials, plus concessional prices for Soviet oil shipped to the three CMEA developing countries (preferential tariffs for maritime transport might be included in this category as well); the savings in pay for Soviet technical personnel sent to the Third World (they are reportedly being paid less than half the amount received by average Western experts); the value of training local personnel; the amount of scholarships awarded to Third World students;[2] possibly some of the revolving automatic credits granted to cover Third World trade deficits; and commitments instead of actual disbursements (disbursements have run at about 50 percent of commitments in the 1980s).

Some of these items undoubtedly represent an advantage for the recipient country and a drain on Soviet resources. The preferential prices in favor of the three CMEA countries could certainly be considered as gifts. But because the USSR will not release data separated by type of assistance and by country distribution, one must rely on Western estimates. According to the Organization for Economic Cooperation and Development (OECD), the USSR has gradually increased its share in world ODA to the developing countries. In 1987, with $4.3 billion of net disbursements (8.6 percent of the world total), it ranked fifth, behind the United States (17.7 percent), Japan (14.8 percent), France (12.9 percent), and West Germany (8.7 percent).[3] This figure does not automatically give us the exact ODA/

GNP ratio, because estimates of the Soviet GNP vary rather widely. A range of estimates may put such ratio between 0.20 and 0.32 percent, with the upper limit still below the 0.35 percent average of the Western countries and the lower limit on a par with the U.S. level, which at present is one of the lowest.

For Soviet overall net disbursements in the 1980s, estimates in current dollars show an upward trend except for 1982 and 1984 (table 1). This prima facie impression may be misleading. Two distinct periods should be considered, with 1985 as the watershed. Until then, the dollar had been appreciating against the ruble, which depressed the dollar value of flows expressed in the Soviet currency. Because price increases more or less offset the effect of the exchange rate, however, current values can be taken as a correct indicator. By contrast, from 1985 to 1987 the dollar depreciated and, compounded by price increases, increased the value of aid flows. At 1985 prices and exchange rates, the volume of Soviet economic assistance increased only in 1986 (by 6.1 percent), and actually declined in 1987 by 5.6 percent. Although the time span is too short to be statistically significant, the divergent evolution of Soviet aid flows in the first three years under Gorbachev seems nevertheless to signal certain difficulties in the process.

Geographical Distribution of Aid

Political considerations still loom very large in Soviet aid patterns. During 1985–1987, the three CMEA countries obtained an average of 65.3 percent of total gross bilateral disbursements (excluding scholarships), three other socialist countries (Kampuchea, Laos, and North Korea) obtained 7.7 percent, the six socialist-oriented countries obtained 9.6 percent, and the remaining 17.4 percent is mostly India's (13.2 percent) (table 2).

According to the evidence of this three-year period, Gorbachev does not appear to have drastically reoriented

TABLE 1
Estimated Soviet Net Disbursements to the Developing Countries, 1980-1987
($ millions)

1980	1981	1982	1983	1984	1985	1986	1987	1986*	1987*
2,313	2,558	2,504	3,046	2,889	3,099	3,991	4,321	3,288	3,105

*Adjusted by author; 1985 prices and exchange rates.

Source: Organization for Economic Cooperation and Development, Development Co-operation (1987 and 1988 Report), Paris, December 1987 and 1988.

his aid policy. Something is happening, however, inside the various countries. Because it receives more than one-third of total Soviet aid, Vietnam firmly outweighs Mongolia and Cuba. The USSR's pledge to double assistance to Vietnam seems to be at work. Mongolia is also receiving increasing amounts of aid, according to a Soviet promise to increase assistance by 50 percent in the current quinquennium. Things do not appear as bright for Cuba, although it received a similar pledge. In constant prices, Soviet gross disbursements diminished by 41.5 percent in 1986 and slightly recovered the following year, although at a lower volume than in 1985. A similar pattern is evident at the moment in the cases of Laos, North Korea, Afghanistan, and Nicaragua (table 3).

Three points deserve to be highlighted as far as the nonsocialist developing countries are concerned. First, India's role has been greatly enhanced under Gorbachev, paralleling its rank as top trading partner of the Soviet Union in the nonsocialist Third World. Huge credits amounting to more than $4 billion were extended to the Asian country during 1985-1987, covering a broad range of sectors such as power generation, nonferrous metallurgy, oil exploration, coal mining, the modernization of the Bokaro steel mill, and a refinery. During Gorbachev's November 1988 visit to India, new major credits valued at R 3.2 billion

TABLE 2
Estimated Soviet Gross Bilateral Disbursements by Average Share and Rank (excluding scholarships), 1985–1987

Country/Country Group	Percent Share	Rank
CMEA developing countries	65.3	
Vietnam	34.3	1
Mongolia	16.4	2
Cuba	14.6	3
Other Socialist countries	7.7	
Kampuchea	3.2	6
Laos	2.3	7
North Korea	2.2	8
Nonsocialist developing countries	27.0	
Socialist-oriented countries	9.6	
Afghanistan	5.6	5
Nicaragua	1.4	9
Mozambique	1.2	12
South Yemen	0.7	13
Ethiopia	0.5	15
Angola	0.2	19
Other developing countries	17.4	
India	13.2	4
Algeria	1.3	10
Syria	1.3	11
Madagascar	0.6	14
Bangladesh	0.3	16
Sri Lanka	0.3	17
Brazil	0.2	18
Egypt	0.1	20
Tanzania	0.1	21
Guinea	0.02	22

Source: Author's calculations based on estimates published in OECD, *Development Co-operation*, various issues, as well as on personal estimates.

TABLE 3
Estimated Soviet Gross Disbursements, 1985–1987
($ millions)

Country/Category	1985	1986	1987	1986*	1987*
Cuba	655	532	656	383	400
Mongolia	550	706	804	581	588
Vietnam	1,056	1,457	1,811	1,217	1,397
Afghanistan	219	283	200	233	114
Kampuchea	98	150	161	128	123
Laos	99	81	110	58	71
North Korea	96	123	62	101	24
Other developing countries	697	1,063	930	905	657
Scholarships	190	200	220	157	146
Multilateral contributions	4	5	7	4	5
Total	3,664	4,600	4,961	3,767	3,525

*Adjusted by author; 1985 prices and exchange rates.

Source: OECD, *Development Co-operation* (1988 Report), Paris, December 1988.

(about $2 billion) were announced for two 1,000 megawatt (MW) nuclear power stations and Soviet-aided thermal and hydro projects. For economic as well as political and strategic reasons, India continues to be a close economic partner of the Soviet Union.

Second, a $60 million loan was extended to Brazil for a steel alloy plant in 1987, followed by an agreement in 1988 on two projects concerning a railway line and an irrigation project. This first concessional loan ever accorded to Brazil seems to indicate the Soviets wish to establish closer economic ties with moderate developing countries that are large and potentially wealthy.

Finally, Egypt's reappearance on the scene is worth noting. The Arab country had not received aid from the USSR since the early 1970s. In 1987 it obtained a $29 million loan for steel hot-rolling plants, while in 1988 rumor had it that the Soviet Union was willing to extend a long-term loan of $2.4 billion for about 40 projects. In the meantime, Egypt obtained the rescheduling of its military debt, estimated at $2 to $3 billion. On the whole, Gorbachev's economic activism spans the three continents as it focuses on selected Third World partners.

The Debt Problem

How much indebtedness has this flow of credits induced for the developing countries? Soviet scholars privately indicate a figure of R 15 billion (roughly $23.7 billion) for the nonsocialist Third World civilian debt; although no estimates exist for the socialist developing countries, their debt is said to be much higher.

On top of all this, the USSR is left with rather conspicuous military credits. According to unofficial Soviet estimates, nonsocialist Third World outstanding military debts are in the range of $59 billion – that is, two-and-a-half times the civilian debt. When and how much of this will be repaid is an open question.

Although repayments can be made in kind, many countries have not been able to repay their debts to the Soviet Union. The CMEA countries, as well as other socialist and socialist-oriented countries, are often indicated in the Soviet scholarly community as bad payers. But other countries, such as Peru, Zambia, and Madagascar, seem to be on the blacklist as well. During the 1980s, average repayments from nonsocialist countries have been two to three-and-a-half times higher than those from the socialist Third World. The ratio of repayments to gross disbursements for the first group of countries was 40 percent in the first half of the 1980s, rising to 51 percent in 1985–1987; in comparison, the ratios for those periods were 7 percent and 5 percent respectively for the socialist developing countries.

Soviet positions on indebtedness have evolved over time. Practice has preceded official pronouncements. Until the mid-1980s, the USSR usually did not grant debt-relief measures. Since 1985, debt rescheduling and relief have been applied to various countries, such as Afghanistan, Cuba, Egypt, Ethiopia, Madagascar, Mozambique, Peru, South Yemen, Syria, and Zambia. The possibility of transforming debts into equity shares (debt-equity swaps) in joint ventures that produce for the Soviet market is being thoroughly examined by Soviet specialists in the cases of Cuba, Ghana, Mongolia, Mozambique, Nigeria, Peru, and Vietnam.

Official Soviet pronouncements have also changed notably. They usually have consisted of verbal support for Third World demands, with no indication of practical measures. Currently the USSR is stating its readiness to cancel the debt of least-developed countries (or to declare a moratorium for 100 years) and to support proposals to reduce debt by 30 percent. The USSR is also stating that it is in favor of market-oriented solutions to the problem. Like the Western creditors, the Soviet Union might as well begin to recognize that there is no alternative to the debt problem but partial forgiveness.

The Quality of Economic Assistance

A discussion of the quality of aid often refers to financial terms as well as other pertinent conditions. The *financial terms* of Soviet assistance in the 1980s consisted mostly of development loans extended at interest rates oscillating between 2 and 5 percent, with a repayment period of 10 to 15 years and a grace period of 3 to 5 years. This yields a grant element of approximately 50 percent, as compared with roughly 90 percent in the loans of Western countries. An Indian source rather sympathetic to the cause of Indo-Soviet economic relations reveals that the interest rate obtained on loans received by India in the 1980–1981 period was the following: Canada and the Organization of Petroleum Exporting Countries (OPEC) – interest-free; International Development Assistance (IDA), IMF, and the Federal Republic of Germany – less than 1 percent; the USSR, Austria, the Netherlands, and the United States – 2 to 2.5 percent; France, Japan, and the International Bank for Reconstruction and Development (IBRD) – about 2.5 percent.[4]

It should be noted here that interest rates are, in general, set higher for the nonsocialist Third World, except in a few cases, such as India. In recent years, a larger share of commodity aid might have raised the Soviet grant element. According to a recent Soviet official declaration, in 1986–1987 the average rate of interest was 1.8 percent, the average maturity 15.5 years, and the grace period 4 years, which raises the concessionality of total net assistance to 91.6 percent.[5]

It should be remembered that both OECD and Soviet estimates calculate the grant element from dollar interest rates converted into ruble rates at the unrealistic dollar-ruble official exchange rate. The artificial overvaluation of the ruble may thus greatly overstate the Soviet grant element. Whatever its exact value, the grant element in Soviet aid could well decline if the new trend of harder terms in commercial credits asserts itself.

A fundamental element in evaluating the *conditions* of aid is the extent to which the assistance is tied to buying in the donor country or to buying of specific goods and services. Here the difference between the USSR and the West is considerable. The amount of Western aid tied to buying ranges from 20 to 70 percent, depending on the country. Soviet assistance is almost entirely tied. Except for a minor quantity of convertible currency loans, Soviet credits do not consist of financial flows, but of flows of goods and services – mostly machinery and equipment, feasibility studies, geological prospecting, and construction works. This "naturalization" of assistance finds its counterpart in debt repayments, which consist mostly of traditional export goods or of products issued from the assistance projects. In this way, the USSR secures an outlet for its equipment and at the same time a source for long-term supplies of some essential products, mainly raw materials and agricultural products, but also several consumer goods. On the other side, the developing countries are able to develop their resources without paying in convertible currencies. Only occasionally are there certain clauses that oblige the recipient country to pay the balance in convertible currency at the end of the year; moreover, Soviet technicians must be paid in hard currency and their necessities provided for in local currency.

Another traditional feature of Soviet assistance is the relative paucity of food aid; in 1987 food accounted for less than 0.5 percent of total assistance flows, as compared with an average of almost 7 percent for Western countries. A case in point was the drought in Ethiopia at the beginning of the 1980s, when Soviet food aid represented a mere 2 percent of Western contributions. In view of its own "food problem," this amount is not surprising, although recently the Soviet Union had to provide increased amounts of food to Nicaragua, Mozambique, South Yemen, and Ethiopia.

Finally, Soviet aid is traditionally almost entirely *bilateral*, its multilateral assistance amounting to a sheer 0.1 percent in 1987 (against an average of 27.8 percent for Western countries). Here, too, there are signs of a changing Soviet attitude. In 1987 and 1988, the USSR took part as observer in the meetings of the Asian Development Bank and the Southern African Development Co-ordinating Conference, expressing the intention to become a donor member in both. It has also pledged a contribution to the Africa Fund of the Non-Aligned Movement and in July 1987 signed an agreement for the Common Fund for Commodities by subscribing 6 percent. A reorientation toward more multilateral assistance seems to be under way.

Soviet assistance has traditionally concentrated on big industrial projects in the state sector, especially in heavy industry and energy. Although small compared with Western aid, Soviet assistance at times has been crucial to the

development of the infrastructure as well as the heavy industry of some Third World countries, notably India. This
assistance model seems to have lost its popularity, however.
Some indications of a changing distribution of aid by sector
can be detected here too. The USSR does not release figures
on the value of assistance provided to the different sectors
of Third World economies. The Soviet statistical yearbook
does publish data, however, on the number and types of
projects built in developing countries. According to this
volume, between 1985 and 1987 the share of industry and
transport has slightly declined in favor of agriculture, hous-
ing, and education.[6]

Renewed Emphasis on Efficiency

The drain on domestic resources represented by assistance
to the Third World, particularly to the three CMEA developing countries, is encountering growing criticism in the
USSR. The Soviets are not satisfied with the way in which
aid is either administered by their authorities or is used by
the recipient countries. Disenchantment is no less acute on
the other side.

Devastating criticisms have started to appear in specialized Soviet journals. In a recent article, two Soviet econ-
omists indicate the reasons for ineffective cooperation with
Cuba, Mongolia, and Vietnam. Both the Soviet organizations and the recipient countries are under fire. The authors
argue that (1) in many cases aid has been oriented toward
such heavy resource-intensive industry as the mining and
power sectors, with scarce attention paid to such sectors as
agriculture, light industry, and the social infrastructure.
They particularly criticize the tendency to build large projects that lead to a protracted freezing of resources and a
diversion of resources from other sectors of the economy.
Instead, they advocate small-sized projects with a quick
economic return. (2) The feasibility studies of many projects
are also questioned. The authors underline especially the

scant attention paid to the supplying of raw materials and manpower to future projects, to the domestic demand for products, and to the quality of final products. (3) Inadequate scientific and technological assistance is one of the major reasons that many projects operate under capacity (in Mongolia one-fifth are believed to be operating at 70 percent of their capacity). (4) Soviet enterprises and organizations show little interest in the results of the projects. (5) Finally, aid is viewed as a unilateral, obligatory burden, with little expectation of obtaining higher returns.

Criticism of the way Soviet aid is utilized by recipient countries is no milder. Another article criticizes the tardy commissioning of project construction and the irrational distribution of Soviet products in Vietnam.[8] The Vietnamese seem to be conscious of the problem. At the forty-third CMEA session in 1987, the head of the Vietnamese delegation noted that aid was not used effectively enough. Mongolia does not fare much better. Its enterprises and organizations are accused of ordering too much equipment and too many machines and spare parts; an unused stock of parts accumulated to the extent that Mongolian specialists have advocated stricter control over the effective use of imported equipment. Cuba is frequently criticized for not completing projects before undertaking new ones.

For a few years now, the USSR has been actively pressing within the CMEA for the three CMEA developing countries to restructure their economies, thereby incorporating themselves more fully in the international socialist division of labor.[9] The following areas of development have priority: Cuba—the agro-industrial complex; Mongolia—agriculture, mineral raw materials, light industry, and food; and Vietnam—agriculture and light industry. If developed, all sectors would better satisfy the needs of the more industrialized members. Another line of Soviet action is to press the East European members of the CMEA to share more equally the burden of aid, with the USSR providing at present 89 percent of total CMEA net ODA disbursements. At the forty-third and forty-fourth sessions of the CMEA in 1987 and 1988, donor countries agreed to elaborate a new multi-lateral approach to assistance and to make their relations with the three less-developed members more commercial.

Such tougher, more businesslike attitudes are also discernible in relations with other friendly socialist-oriented states. At the end of 1987, a Soviet official told Nicaraguan authorities that Soviet aid could be more efficiently used. In the new cooperation agreement of 1988, the amount of aid is lower than in the previous agreement. Afghanistan, Ethiopia, and even Guinea were pressed to give more room to the private sector in their economies, while Vietnam was already progressing in that direction. Angola and Mozambique were asked to seek more assistance from Western donors.

Finally, the entire organization of aid is undergoing a profound restructuring. Early in 1988, a new Ministry of Foreign Economic Relations was created by merging the State Committee for Foreign Economic Relations (the former aid agency) and the Ministry of Foreign Trade. The new body now centralizes all matters related to aid. At the same time, considerable attention is paid to long-term cooperation programs, a framework integrating trade exchanges and national plans and aiming at the stability and development of new forms of economic cooperation. Thirteen developing countries have already signed similar documents.

Ministerial reorganization is not synonymous with increased efficiency, however. Lack of coordination and of experienced staff, plus the permanence of old-style bureaucrats well entrenched in strategic posts abroad, are considerable obstacles.

In conclusion, the new pragmatism of the Soviet leadership expresses itself in three fundamental directions: (1) when the level of assistance cannot be lowered for political and strategic reasons, the USSR fosters the restructuring of local economies toward a better meeting of Soviet needs and a thriftier use of resources; (2) it shows more caution in sustaining new friends and presses them to search for other sources of assistance; and (3) it is inclined to choose the more industrialized representatives within the nonsocialist Third World. Soviet aid policy is thus increasingly geared to win better economic returns for the USSR, a trend now apparent in its trade policy as well.

3

The Geographical Orientation
of Trade

Trade with the developing countries amounts to roughly one-fifth of the USSR's total imports and well over one-
quarter of its exports. Within this overall value, however,
one should distinguish two different – and, until recently,
almost equivalent in value – components: the share of the
socialist developing countries, which has been rather stable
at 12 to 14 percent of overall trade in the 1980s, and the
share of the nonsocialist Third World – the only part of the
world known as the "developing countries" in Soviet
literature.

The imports from nonsocialist developing countries,
which accounted for an average of 11 to 12 percent of total
imports in the first five years of the 1980s, fell to a historic
low of 7.8 percent in 1986–1987. In comparison, the share of
global exports of these countries reversed its downward tendency in the first period – from a peak of 16 percent to a
trough of 13 percent – to reach 14 percent in the following
two years. Some caution is needed here, because these
shares are calculated from current values, which may be
affected by the different evolutions of prices in the world.
And the volume index published by the USSR cannot be
used to deflate such values; since 1982 it no longer distin-
guishes between exports and imports. My own estimates in

volume terms show that between 1980 and 1986 Soviet exports to the Third World increased by 34.7 percent, and imports increased by 20.2 percent (chapter 4, table 7). The gap between the higher level of exports and the lower level of imports might then have increased in the period under consideration.

Until now, this discussion has referred to the overall value of trade with nonsocialist developing countries as reported by the Soviet foreign trade yearbook. Yet the total value of reported exports and imports is always greater than the sum of exports and imports for the individual countries belonging to the group. This unspecified *residue* or remainder is really minor in the case of imports and very likely corresponds to some partners not listed in the foreign trade yearbook but usually accounted for by international agencies (Hong Kong, Gabon, Kenya, Réunion, Jamaica, Mauritius, Dominican Republic, and others – all together accounting for not more than $100 million a year), plus some strategic materials from the identified countries. By comparison, the value of the residue unidentified by countries of destination in Soviet exports is much larger, reaching at present a peak of more than one-half of reported exports to the nonsocialist Third World. Western experts, as well as some Soviet scholars in private, generally assume that most of it consists of arms shipments (which by no means should be confined to these figures), while a lesser part concerns strategic materials and other trade partners.[1] Suffice it to say for now that without these sales, the picture of Soviet exports would appear much gloomier.

A Systems Approach to Trade Analysis

When grouped together, by systems, the eight socialist developing countries had a share of Soviet global exports to the Third World that was very high during 1980–1985, ranging from 44 to 48 percent, a large part of which (27 to 28 percent) was from the three CMEA developing countries (table 4). This strong political orientation of Soviet exports,

TABLE 4
Distribution of Soviet Trade with the Developing Countries
(shares as a percentage of the total)

	1980	1981	1982	1983	1984	1985	1986	1987
Exports								
CMEA developing countries	26.7	27.5	27.0	27.9	28.1	30.8	32.9	31.2
Other socialist developing countries	20.0	17.3	16.6	17.5	19.5	21.7	18.8	18.9
Nonsocialist developing countries (total reported)	53.6	55.2	56.4	54.7	53.8	47.5	50.2	49.9
Socialist-oriented countries	4.0	4.6	4.3	5.2	6.5	6.9	6.8	6.2
Other countries (identified)	25.7	27.9	25.9	22.5	20.8	19.5	14.5	15.5
Residue	23.9	22.7	26.2	27.0	26.9	21.1	28.9	28.2
Residue as % of total reported exports to nonsocialist developing countries	44.7	40.6	46.2	48.7	50.7	43.7	57.6	55.3

Imports

CMEA developing countries	24.3	18.5	24.5	24.6	26.9	28.2	33.5	36.2
Other socialist developing countries	22.9	23.4	24.7	21.6	23.8	27.0	30.1	25.9
Nonsocialist developing countries (total reported)	52.8	58.2	50.8	53.8	49.3	44.8	36.4	37.9
Socialist-oriented countries	3.2	2.6	2.3	2.3	2.2	2.2	2.2	2.3
Other countries (identified)	48.4	54.5	47.4	50.0	46.4	42.0	33.0	34.6
Residue	1.2	1.1	1.1	1.5	0.7	0.6	1.2	1.0
Residue as % of total reported imports from nonsocialist developing countries	2.3	1.8	2.1	2.8	1.4	1.3	3.3	2.6

Note: CMEA developing countries = Cuba, Mongolia, and Vietnam; other socialist developing countries = China, North Korea, Yugoslavia, Kampuchea, and Laos; socialist-oriented countries = Afghanistan, Angola, Ethiopia, Mozambique, Nicaragua, and South Yemen.

Source: Calculated from *Vneshniaya Torgovlia SSSR v . . . g: Statisticheskii sbornik* [Foreign trade of the USSR for the year . . .: Statistical compendium] (Moscow: Finansi i statistika, various years).

which partly reflects Soviet aid policy, has not changed under Gorbachev. Statistical evidence available for the past three years shows, if anything, an enlarged share for the CMEA countries. Cuba alone accounts for almost one-fifth of total reported Soviet exports to the Third World.

An opposite pattern is noticeable in the shares of total exports to the nonsocialist Third World. The socialist-oriented countries have reached a level of 7 percent – mostly because of Afghanistan – although a slight decrease is noticeable since 1985.[2] Beginning in 1981, exports identified by countries of destination (mostly civilian exports) have diminished in relative importance (barring a recent slight pickup), while the residue (mostly military sales) has increased in importance. Since 1981, the residue has always been larger than exports to identified countries. In 1987 it amounted to more than 28 percent of total exports to the Third World and 55 percent of reported exports to the nonsocialist developing countries.

Socialist countries account for more than 60 percent of Soviet imports from the Third World, with more than half of it attributable to the three CMEA countries. Conversely, the nonsocialist Third World does not even reach 40 percent, down from well over 50 percent at the beginning of the decade. Two provisos are pertinent, however. First, the countries with socialist orientation are far less present on the import than on the export side, accounting for roughly 2 percent of global imports. This is logical, because exports reflect Soviet aid to these countries. Second, the residue, too, is minimal, hovering around the same level. As a consequence, the share of imports from the identified nonsocialist countries is much higher than on the export side – roughly 34 percent as opposed to 15 percent.

Trade Analysis by Economic Criteria

Further analysis of Soviet trade distribution with the nonsocialist Third World is only possible by excluding the residue. From now on, this discussion shall refer only to Soviet trade identified by countries of origin or destination (mostly civilian trade), with the understanding that most of the export residue probably is attributable to Middle Eastern countries.

What type of country does the USSR prefer as a trading partner? An analysis of the developing world by the category of *income* reveals that the USSR today imports relatively more from, and exports relatively less to, high-income countries – that is, countries with a gross domestic product or GDP of more than $1500 per capita (table 5). The reverse is true for low-income countries. The dynamics of the 1980s are very revealing in this context. At the beginning of the decade, when the export receipts of richer partners (mostly Middle Eastern oil producers) were plentiful, their relative share in Soviet exports was the highest. In 1982–1983, when balance of payments difficulties started depressing their global imports, their share of Soviet exports correspondingly declined. Since 1983 the share of the lowest income economies has always been the largest (more than 50 percent since 1984). The picture looks rather different on the import side. Here the richer countries always obtained the highest share (in fact more than 50 percent until 1985). The decline in the price of oil, although depressing the value of imports, did not imperil this position, for one reason because of the growing volume of Soviet imports of oil for re-export.

An analysis of the developing countries by the category of *major export* immediately highlights the insignificance of major exporters of manufacturers to Soviet exports. Of the six major newly industrializing countries (NICs), only Argentina, Brazil, and Singapore appear in the Soviet foreign trade yearbook. According to the UN COMTRADE Data Bank, Hong Kong's total trade turnover with the USSR is roughly $100 million a year. No direct trade has been conducted until now with South Korea and Taiwan. The USSR sells mostly raw materials and intermediate goods to the three identified NICs. The importance of the NICs is much larger in Soviet imports. The Soviet Union

TABLE 5
Distribution of Soviet Identified Trade with the Nonsocialist Developing Countries by Economic Criteria and Share of the First Ten Partners, 1980–1987 (percentage of total)

	Exports								Imports							
	1980	1981	1982	1983	1984	1985	1986	1987	1980	1981	1982	1983	1984	1985	1986	1987
Income category[a]																
More than US $1500	35.4	40.7	45.9	34.2	24.8	23.1	22.9	23.0	51.3	57.7	56.8	64.9	62.9	57.8	47.6	49.3
US $500–1500	23.5	23.4	19.4	24.0	23.3	23.4	17.7	19.8	18.8	16.7	11.8	11.0	12.0	14.0	15.6	16.5
Less than US $500	41.1	35.8	34.7	41.8	51.9	53.5	59.4	57.2	29.9	25.6	31.4	24.1	25.1	28.2	36.8	34.2
Major export category																
Petroleum[b]	36.5	43.6	45.8	38.8	26.2	23.7	23.9	22.5	18.6	16.8	26.5	32.9	37.9	34.2	36.3	32.2
Manufactures[c]	1.8	1.9	4.4	2.9	2.7	2.7	2.7	2.8	29.8	39.0	26.2	27.2	22.6	22.4	9.8	15.5
Share of the first 10 partners in total identified trade with the nonsocialist Third World																
World	77.7	78.4	78.0	73.7	71.1	74.0	78.2	83.3	76.7	83.7	86.9	84.5	78.9	80.5	80.0	83.0

Source: Calculated from *Vneshniaya Torgovlia SSSR v . . . g* (various years).

a. Income category based on US $ GDP per capita.
b. Major petroleum exporters = the OPEC countries plus Angola, the Congo, Mexico, and Syria.
c. Major exporters of manufactures = Argentina, Brazil, and Singapore (Hong Kong does not appear in *Vneshniaya Torgovlia*, and South Korea and Taiwan do not trade directly with the USSR).

receives mostly foodstuffs and agricultural products from the two Latin American NICs, with Singapore as the only identified NIC that delivers a larger volume of manufactured products. Manufactured products also constitute the major import from Hong Kong.

Until 1983, major petroleum exporters loomed larger in Soviet exports than in Soviet imports; since then the reverse is true for the reasons explained above. Today they account for roughly one-third of Soviet imports and for slightly over one-fifth of Soviet exports.

Trade by Regions and Individual Countries

The direction of Soviet trade can also be detected on a *regional* level. Asian countries have always been the privileged source of supply and, since 1983, of exports as well. Today these countries represent a share in Soviet imports of 37 percent and a share in Soviet exports of 46 percent. The Middle East lost its rank of first place in Soviet exports after 1982, but has recently increased its importance as a source of supply (roughly one-quarter on each side), for reasons briefly touched upon above. Africa comes third. At the beginning of the 1970s, Africa represented almost 45 percent of Soviet trade with the Third World; it steadily lost ground during the 1970s, falling to just over one-fifth of Soviet trade in 1987. Last is Latin America; it was a dynamic market for Soviet imports until 1981 (40 percent, mostly owing to Argentinian cereals), but declined to 17 percent in 1987. Soviet exports have not encountered great success in penetrating this market, although the share is at present higher than in 1980 (8.7 percent as opposed to 2.7 percent).

Global and regional analyses are largely insufficient in discussing Soviet trade with the Third World, because Soviet commercial relations follow the ups and downs of its relations with individual countries. A clear example is the sharp cut in imports from Argentina in 1986, which contributed to more than half of the reduction of total Soviet imports from the Third World during that year.

Soviet trade has traditionally been highly concentrated: 83 percent of its exports and imports are taken by 10 countries, and since 1984 the concentration index has tended to increase. In 1987 the first three partners took 49 percent of Soviet exports and supplied 51 percent of its imports from the nonsocialist Third World (table 6).

The composition of the first 10 partners has changed slightly over time. Algeria, Angola, and Nicaragua, among the top export partners in 1987, were not included in 1980, while Algeria and Turkey are newcomers on the import side. This shifting of trade relations has taken place around a solid nucleus of stable partners. The leader is India, which has held its top position for the past 20 years. Today it takes 28 percent of Soviet exports to the nonsocialist Third World and supplies 24 percent of Soviet imports – in absolute values, roughly $1.7 billion each way. If the socialist countries are also taken into account, India ranks fourth in Soviet exports (on a par with Vietnam and after Cuba and Yugoslavia) and third in Soviet imports (again after Cuba and Yugoslavia).

Among the top ten partners, six other countries appear both on the export and on the import side. Two of them (Afghanistan and Turkey) are bordering countries, three (Iraq, Syria, and Egypt) are Middle Eastern countries, and one (Algeria) is an African country. The three remaining countries on each side are a clear example of the difference noted earlier between Soviet imports and exports: on the import side, Argentina and Brazil (food and agricultural products) and Libya (oil); on the export side, Angola, Ethiopia, and South Yemen, all socialist-oriented countries. Overall a unique rationale for trade does not seem to exist: economic supply needs are determined by geographic proximity, strategic considerations, and political motivations (political motivations seem to be more numerous on the export side).

TABLE 6
**Share of the First Ten Partners in Soviet Identified Trade
with the Nonsocialist Developing Countries, 1987**

	Exports		*Imports*	
Partner	*Percent share*	*Partner*		*Percent share*
India	27.8	India		23.9
Afghanistan	13.5	Iraq		17.5
Iraq	8.1	Argentina		9.3
Egypt	7.4	Egypt		6.6
Syria	6.3	Libya		5.7
Nicaragua	5.2	Brazil		5.6
Turkey	5.0	Afghanistan		5.2
Ethiopia	3.8	Syria		4.2
Algeria	3.3	Algeria		2.5
Angola	2.9	Turkey		2.5
Share of the first 3 partners	49.4			50.7
Share of the first 5 partners	63.1			63.0
Share of the first 10 partners	83.3			83.0

Note: "Identified trade" excludes the residue.

Source: Calculated from *Vneshniaya Torgovlia SSSR v 1987 g.*

The importance of single developing countries to Soviet world trade is very low except for Cuba (whose share is roughly 6 percent), followed by Yugoslavia (3.1 percent), India (1.7 percent), and China (1.2 percent). By comparison, the Soviet share of the foreign trade of individual countries is, in some cases, rather large. Such is the case of the three CMEA countries (90 percent of Mongolian trade is with the Soviet Union as is 70 percent of both Cuban and Vietnamese trade) and Yugoslavia (40 percent). As for the nonsocialist countries, import dependency on the USSR was higher in 1986 for Afghanistan (91 percent), Angola (32 percent), South Yemen (30 percent), Nicaragua (21 percent), and Ethiopia (20 percent), followed by Syria (15 percent) and India (9 percent). On the other hand, the USSR was a major outlet for the exports of some Third World countries in the same year (1986): Afghanistan (65 percent), then South Yemen (24 percent), India and Syria (19 percent), Argentina (17 percent), Egypt (13 percent) (calculated from the *UN Monthly Bulletin of Statistics*, July and August 1988). Compared to Third World ties with the West, trade dependency vis-à-vis the Soviet Union involves a rather restricted number of countries. Moreover, some of the nonsocialist countries involved – India, Syria, and even Angola and Ethiopia – have well-established links with Western enterprises.

A New Direction for Soviet Trade

The geographical trade pattern that emerges from the statistical data available does not seem to conform to the new Soviet strategy toward the Third World. Yet the new attitude toward developing countries combined with economic reforms must affect the direction of trade sooner or later. The newly granted right for Soviet enterprises to trade directly with foreign partners and to retain most of the convertible currency earnings will probably push the Soviets toward richer partners, with little regard for foreign policy objectives. (The Soviets see these richer partners as alternative suppliers to the West.) As just discussed, the Asian NICs, particularly South Korea and Taiwan, are almost entirely absent from Soviet trade. Soviet scholars are very aware that Asia is today the world's most dynamic region and that the four Asian NICs have emerged as important buyers and sellers of manufactures. As a result, the scant development of ties seems all the more irrational.

Soviet research institutes have been asked to formulate a policy of trade reorientation toward the Asian NICs, particularly South Korea. At the same time, a new Committee for Asian-Pacific Co-operation was set up in March 1988, headed by Evgenii Primakov, a director of the USSR Academy of Sciences. In a speech given in the Soviet city of Krasnoyarsk in September 1988, Gorbachev enumerated a series of measures to intensify economic cooperation in the Asian-Pacific region — for example, special economic zones in the Soviet Far East, with a preferential customs and taxation regime for joint ventures and special advantages for Soviet enterprises.[3]

The Soviet Far East is a resource-rich but undeveloped region. South Korea (along with Japan) is seen as the likeliest source of technology and credits necessary to exploit the existing mineral resources. Recent initiatives seem to confirm this move. In October 1988 the USSR signed a memorandum on further cooperation with South Korea; in December South Korean construction companies were invited to bid for a contract to build a trade center in Nakhodka, a Soviet Far East city near Vladivostock. In January 1989, the South Korean corporation Hyundai was reported to be negotiating a Soviet order of nine ships and studying the possibility of building an oil pipeline to connect Siberia to the two Koreas.[4]

Direct trade relations with Taiwan may not be too far away either. Since March 1988, Taiwan has established direct trade links with East European countries, while keeping indirect trade with the USSR, China, and Vietnam. Barring political recognition, which would be opposed by China, economic ties between the USSR and Taiwan could soon become a reality. Soviet officials have repeatedly disclosed that both Taiwan and South Korea are considered to be important suppliers of computer components, as well as parts for other high-tech industries.

The other aspect of Gorbachev's Asian economic policy has been the attempt to establish better links with such ASEAN countries as Indonesia, Malaysia, the Philippines, and Thailand. Mutual visits of commercial delegations have been taking place since 1986.

The Latin American NICs are also increasingly courted. There are many proposals for pursuing trade and joint ventures with Brazil, the region's giant and the USSR's preferred partner in that part of the globe. Finally, Soviet initiatives toward the oil-rich Gulf countries should be noted. Besides diplomatically recognizing Oman and the UAE, the USSR in 1987 agreed with Kuwait to pursue some joint ventures and mutually serve each other's oil markets in Europe, Africa, and Asia. And in 1988 it agreed with Abu Dhabi to cooperate in the field of banking (with a $50 million loan from two Abu Dhabi banks as a start).

4

The Commodity Composition
of Trade

Trade between the USSR and the Third World has a classical North-South structure (save some rare exceptions mentioned later).[1] The USSR has tended to see the developing countries as a source of food and raw materials and as an outlet for its manufactures. Food and raw materials were 82 percent of Soviet identified imports in 1986, with food accounting for almost 60 percent (table 7). This share has somewhat decreased during the 1980s, but its amount is still very large, indicating the USSR's interests and especially its food crisis. The share of agricultural products and fuels imported by the Soviet Union during the same period shows a larger than average increase in volume. The same applies to manufactured goods, which are, however, still at a rather low level (18 percent) compared with their level in North-South trade. Manufactured goods accounted for 47 percent of the Western countries' imports from the Third World in 1986.

The opposite picture emerges when Soviet exports are examined (tables 7 and 8). It is difficult to ascertain the precise Soviet export structure because of the overall export residue mentioned in chapter 3. The majority of the residue is assumed to be military equipment, which would increase the commodity group "manufactured goods" to

43

TABLE 7

Structure of Soviet Identified Trade with the Third World, 1980 and 1986 (in percent)

	Soviet Exports				Soviet Imports			
	1980	1986 (current prices)	1986 (1980 prices)	Volume increase	1980	1986 (current prices)	1986 (1980 prices)	Volume increase
All food items (SITC 0+1+22+4)	8.1	7.5	7.9	+32.2	67.2	58.8	60.6	+8.6
Agricultural raw materials (SITC 2-22-27-28)	7.1	6.1	7.0	+33.1	7.0	7.4	7.6	+30.7
Ores, metals, crude fertilizers (SITC 27+28+68)	8.2	5.8	6.3	+20.7	5.3	4.3	5.0	+13.2
Fuels (SITC 3)	28.0	26.2	32.1	+54.3	9.1	11.3	12.4	+63.3

Manufactured goods (SITC 5 to 8–68)	48.6	54.4	46.7	+29.2	11.4	18.3	14.4	+51.3
Machinery & transport equipment (SITC 7)	33.7	38.0	32.6	+30.4	0.5	3.8	3.0	+583.7
Total	100.0	100.0	100.0	+34.7	100.0	100.0	100.0	+20.2

Note: SITC = Standard International Trade Classification. "Identified trade" excludes the residue.

Source: Author's estimates based on the *UN Monthly Bulletin of Statistics*, May 1988, and *Vneshniaya Torgovlia SSSR v 1986 g.* Data in current dollars for 1986 were adjusted, taking into account price changes for the different groups of products. Moreover, data for Yugoslavia were subtracted from the totals of 1986 in current dollars given by the *Bulletin*, because these are not comparable with the 1980 totals, where Yugoslavia is not included. Data for this country were estimated by the author from *Vneshniaya Torgovlia*. Given the weight of Soviet trade with Yugoslavia, this would bias the results since, for example, the share of manufactured goods imported by the USSR would shoot up to well over 35 percent. In 1986, Yugoslavia by itself had delivered to the Soviet Union 73 percent more manufactured products in value than all the nonsocialist Third World plus Cuba. The latter are, in fact, the countries included by the UN under the heading "developing market economies," for which global data are given. Usual caveats should apply for such highly aggregated figures.

TABLE 8
Structure of Soviet Exports to the Third World,
1980 and 1986
(in percent)

	1980	1986 (current prices)	1986 (1980 prices)
All food items (SITC 0+1+22+4)	5.6	4.8	5.1
Agricultural raw materials (SITC 2-22-27-28)	4.9	3.9	4.5
Ores, metals, crude fertilizers (SITC 27+28+68)	5.7	3.7	4.0
Fuels (SITC 3)	19.3	16.6	20.6
Manufactured goods (SITC 5 to 8−68)	33.6	34.5	30.0
Machinery and equipment (SITC 7)	23.3	24.1	20.9
Residue*	30.9	36.5	35.8

*Volume increase of the residue, 1980–1986=67.8 percent.

Note: SITC=Standard International Trade Classification.

Source: See table 7. The residue was calculated from *Vneshniaya Torgovlia SSSR v 1980 and 1986 g*. The value of the residue in 1986 was deflated by the same rate as the manufactured goods, assuming that the majority of the unidentified residue consists of military equipment.

more than 70 percent in 1986, up from roughly 65 percent in 1980.

The unspecified residue is the category growing the fastest in volume, pushing military sales as a share of Soviet exports into first place, before civilian manufactured goods. In 1980 civilian manufactured goods still had a higher value than military sales (table 8). Considering only identified (civilian) trade, manufactured goods are the largest commodity group in Soviet exports, amounting to almost 55 percent in 1986, of which 38 percent was represented by machinery and equipment (table 7). The group's real growth has been less dynamic than the average, however. The same is true for all other commodity groups except for fuels. Fuels are the second fastest-growing group in volume (after military sales) and by themselves constitute more than one-quarter of identified Soviet exports to the developing countries.

A country-by-country study reveals another deficiency in Soviet statistics. Aside from the overall residue discussed earlier, other residues appear when each country is analyzed separately. In this type of analysis, unidentified trade appears (1) as the difference between total reported trade with the country in question and the sum of the values of all the commodities reported (intracountry residue), and (2) as the difference between the total reported value of the machinery and equipment group and the sum of the individual items belonging to it (intracommodity residue).

The first 10 Soviet partners in 1987 will be considered in light of these factors. The USSR imports a few products or groups of products almost exclusively from each country; they are nearly always primary products. Fuels constitute the bulk of the imports from Algeria, Libya, Iraq, and Afghanistan. Cereals, soybeans, and seed oils are imported from Argentina; sugar, oil seed meal, and cocoa beans from Brazil; nuts, raw materials, and fertilizers from Turkey; and cotton, oranges, oils, cotton yarn, and cosmetic products from Egypt. The slightly more diversified pattern of imports from Egypt is paralleled by imports from Syria, where more than 80 percent of the identified trade is represented by manufactures and semi-manufactures. In fact, the share of semi-manufactures might be lower because unidentified trade in the amount of 16 percent may well represent nonreported Syrian oil shipments to the USSR. But India is the only Third World country that shows a really diversified structure. Roughly two-thirds of its exports to the USSR cover a broad range of manufactured products, with machinery and equipment accounting for more than one-third.

Of the USSR's socialist partners, only Yugoslavia, an associate member of the CMEA, has a similarly diversified pattern of exports to the USSR. Almost three-quarters of its exports are manufactured goods, with machinery and equipment almost one-half of that amount. North Korea is less diversified, with a large volume of manufactures (roughly 60 percent). China's exports are beginning to be diversified, although they are still concentrated on agricultural products and raw materials. At present, almost one-quarter are manufactures. Imports from Cuba, Mongolia, and Vietnam follow the general Third World pattern, although Vietnam is now selling increasing amounts of light industrial consumer goods to the USSR.[2]

Two items dominate the Soviet export structure with the top 10 nonsocialist partners: (1) machinery and equipment, which range from 50 to 90 percent for most of the countries, except for India and Turkey (roughly 30 percent); and (2) petroleum and petroleum products, which by contrast constitute the highest share of Soviet exports to India (more than one-half), followed by Ethiopia, Nicaragua, and Turkey. Among the socialist countries, Yugoslavia has a pattern similar to India's, while the rest of them resemble the other nonsocialist countries. Finally, unidentified intra-country trade is significant for Syria (25.8 percent) and Afghanistan (15.3 percent), but less so for Angola (9.7 percent), Nicaragua (8.4 percent), and Ethiopia (4.6 percent).

The Soviet Search for Food and Raw Materials

Although food products now constitute the largest share of Soviet imports from the Third World, they have not always done so. In 1950, the USSR was a net exporter of foodstuffs. The situation started deteriorating in the early 1970s with the progressive growth of negative trade balances in this sector.

The general reason for such a prominent role of food in Soviet imports lies in well-known domestic difficulties that hamper Soviet agricultural production. In his speech calling for land leasing in the Soviet countryside, Gorbachev recognized that 6,500 state and collective farms were taking a loss.[3] According to another source, 20 to 30 percent of agricultural products do not reach the consumer because of inadequate storage, lengthy transport, and poor-quality processing.[4] Losses of meat amount to 1 million tons annually, roughly equivalent to 10 percent of its output.[5] The remaining losses are accounted for by inadequate agricultural machinery, scarce spare parts, and lack of incentives.

The Soviet Union imports food from the Third World mainly for two reasons. First, it needs to obtain products that cannot be grown at home – tropical products, for example, that are available mostly in the developing countries and that are becoming more important in the increasingly diversified Soviet diet. Second, the Soviet Union needs alternative sources to Western sellers, as was the case, for example, when it turned to Argentina for cereals after the U.S. embargo on grain in the early 1980s.

Local producers cannot count on Soviet purchases to be stable, however, as demonstrated by the tremendous slash in imported Argentinian grain in 1986. The quality of harvest and price considerations are strong determinants in Soviet behavior, especially if, as was the case, Argentinian grain sells at more than 10 percent above the price of other competitors, has higher transportation costs, and is not accompanied by credit facilities normally granted in the West. When possible, however, Soviet authorities prefer to diversify their imports, as seems to be the case, for instance, in the recent purchase of Saudi Arabian wheat. Instability of Soviet imports, both in quantity and in unit value, has also been found in a wide range of commodities.[6]

The development of agro-industry and the Soviet "Food Program" (approved on May 26, 1982 by the Central Committee of the CPSU to create an integrated agro-industrial complex) should change the composition of food imports to a lower share of cereals and a larger share of tropical products, vegetables, and fruit. Meanwhile, the USSR has come to depend heavily on a few developing countries for selected food products. Almost all soybeans come from China and Argentina; coffee comes from India and Peru; cocoa beans from the Ivory Coast, Ghana, and Brazil; tea from India; sugar from Cuba; rice from India, Thailand, and Burma; oranges from Cuba, Egypt, and Morocco; lemons from Turkey; and dried fruit from Afghanistan. On the other hand, *agricultural raw materials* have become an increasing share of Soviet imports in the 1980s. Here, too, some Third World countries have become important suppliers—such as Indonesia, Malaysia, and Vietnam for natural rubber; Congo, Ivory Coast, and Cameroon for logs of valuable tree species; China and Egypt for cotton fiber; and Bangladesh for jute.

These raw materials are not the only ones needed increasingly for industrial uses. The growing consumption of several *minerals* has not yet been matched by a parallel rise in Soviet production of these minerals. Because it has been the world's largest producer of many minerals and has huge reserves of others, the Soviet Union has long been considered self-sufficient in this sector. It is no longer. In fact, the USSR now depends on foreign supplies for much of its consumption of such important metallic minerals as bauxite-alumina, cobalt, tin, tungsten, and molybdenum, and of such nonmetallic minerals as fluorspar, baryte, and bismuth. Some of them (tungsten, cobalt, and bauxite) are used to produce metals for the armaments industry.

There are various reasons for the shortage of minerals. The quantities produced are not sufficient to meet the abnormally high need. Soviet specialists recognize that the metal-intensity of a unit of national income is twice as large as in the West. Metal waste occurring during the production process can reach one-quarter of all the metal used. Moreover, the mineral content of several ores seems to be decreasing. And the extracting of metal from ore is less efficient than in the West, both for its lower productivity and for the higher amounts of reagents required for processing an identical volume of ore. Finally, the Soviet mineral industry seems to be plagued by increasing costs of exploration and extraction, and the equipment used is often outmoded.[7]

Measures taken in the Soviet Union since 1986–1987 could have ambiguous effects. The emphasis on modernizing existing capacity should improve productivity in mining. In addition, technological progress could lead to growing substitution in the use of some minerals. Yet the upswing of domestic industrial production and the will to satisfy the needs of its CMEA partners should increase Soviet demand for mineral raw materials in the coming years.

Soviet policy on mineral raw materials tends to respond to a double rationale: to fill the gaps created by domestic shortages and to provide substitutes for costlier local extraction and processing. In both instances, it has three striking features: the USSR chooses partners that are generally among the major producers in the world and that seek stable markets and offer high-grade products; it imports minerals preferably in the raw state, or at a very early stage of processing, to minimize the value added in the producing countries; and it tries to avoid payments in convertible currencies by proposing technical assistance or long-term barter agreements.

Under a buy-back agreement, for example (see chapter 6), the USSR imports bauxite from Guinea, which accounts for one-sixth of world production and one-third of the world's high-grade reserves. Bauxite is also imported from Jamaica under a mixed arrangement that provides for an 80 percent payment in convertible currencies and the rest in Lada cars, as well as from Guyana in exchange for Soviet machinery and equipment. And the USSR is giving technical assistance in the building of an alumina plant in India; the assistance is repaid by supplies of alumina and aluminum. Baryte and magnesite are imported from North Korea; cobalt from Cuba and Zambia; fluorspar from Mongolia, China, and Thailand; mica from India; molybdenum from Mongolia; tin ore from Malaysia, Singapore, Laos, and Bolivia; and tungsten from China and Mongolia. Other minerals traded with the socialist Third World, which are in short supply in the USSR, are bought under clearing agreements in most cases. More recent barter deals involve Peruvian minerals, Mozambican nonferrous metal concentrates, and Congolese polymetallic ores (under a buy-back agreement).

The best-known case of Soviet importing of raw materials not in short supply is phosphates. The USSR ranks second in world phosphate production, but production is increasingly costly and insufficient to cover both rapidly rising domestic consumption in agriculture and Eastern European demand. The credit granted to develop phosphate rock deposits at Meskala in Morocco, which has 65 percent of world reserves, should provide considerable rock shipments to the USSR in the future. Meanwhile, another agreement has been concluded with Syria for annual shipments of the same materials in exchange for Soviet technical assistance. A similar example is that of the imports of high-grade manganese concentrates from Gabon. Although the USSR ranks first in world ferromanganese production/exportation, its supply of high-grade ore is rapidly declining.

The Growing Importance of Fuels

In the 1980s, fuels have grown faster in real terms than any other products traded with the Third World except for Soviet imports of Third World machinery and equipment, which started from a very low level (table 7). The fuels consist of mostly petrol, except for Afghan gas piped to the USSR and Soviet gas piped to Yugoslavia (and now beginning to flow to Turkey).

Soviet oil trade with the developing countries cannot be analyzed by itself, but should be considered within the larger context of what I have called the Soviet "oil imbroglio."[8] In the 1980s, fuels have constituted roughly 80 percent of the total earnings (in convertible currencies deriving from Soviet exports to the West) necessary to purchase the advanced technology, the modern equipment, and foodstuffs badly needed by the Soviet economy.[9] At the same time, even larger (although lately diminishing) quantities are shipped to the CMEA partners, constituting one of the chief pillars of what I have called the structure of economic dependence within the CMEA. East European partners, except for Romania, depend almost entirely on Soviet fuel shipments and are increasingly asked to invest in exploiting Soviet deposits.[10]

In 1987, the Western countries took 32 percent of Soviet crude oil exports; 54 percent were destined for Eastern Europe, 8 percent to other socialist countries (mostly to Yugoslavia and Cuba), and 6 percent to the developing countries. Today crude oil exports are just above one-quarter of total identified exports to the Third World. The size of this phenomenon has become apparent in recent years and involves such countries as India, Turkey, Morocco, Brazil, Singapore, Nicaragua, Afghanistan, and Ethiopia. India is by far the leader. In 1987 it received 4.4 million metric tons of crude, roughly similar to the amount West Germany received.

The rationale for Soviet crude oil exports to the Third World seems to be twofold: on the one hand, they are used in the exchange with relatively more advanced developing countries; on the other, the exports are shipped to friendly socialist-oriented countries.

What might at first look surprising, however, is the rising share of fuels in Soviet imports from the Third World, even though the USSR is the world's largest producer of petrol or gas and the second largest exporter of oil.

Gas has been imported for a long time now. Until 1973, the USSR was a net importer of gas. Afghanistan and Iran (until 1980) have provided this fuel through pipelines to

Soviet bordering regions, thus freeing corresponding quantities of Soviet gas for domestic use and for export to Europe. Aside from the prices paid (which Iran and Afghanistan sometimes claimed were lower than those on the world market), the Soviet Union has gained by reducing its investment in transport facilities. Late in 1988, an agreement was reached with Iran to resume Iranian gas deliveries, which had been stopped in 1980 over a pricing dispute.

Until now, the rise of Soviet fuel imports from the Third World during the 1980s was composed entirely of oil, with imports of Afghan gas running at a rather constant level each year. Total quantities of imported crude never stopped increasing from 1981 to 1984 and thereafter tended to be more cyclical. In 1987 they amounted to 14 million metric tons. Various sources of supply have been approached among not only the Soviets' traditional trading partners but also new ones. Saudi Arabia is an example, even though most of its shipments were probably made on behalf of Syria and Iraq in return for Soviet weapons. Algeria, Iraq, Iran, Libya, and Syria have been the main suppliers, while Angola and South Yemen have provided smaller volumes.

Soviet oil imports from the Third World have a particular logic: oil is entirely re-exported – mainly to Western countries but also to Yugoslavia and Romania. Even more remarkably, the rise in imports coincides with declining world oil prices and the USSR's resulting need to channel growing volumes of its crude to convertible currency markets as a way of increasing or at least stabilizing its exports earnings. Until the mid-1980s, imports in value represented on average roughly one-fifth of oil exports to the West. Until 1984, Soviet imports from the Third World contributed to the expansion of export revenues from the West; during the period 1985 to 1986 they prevented export revenues from falling even further. In 1986 and 1987, they accounted for 39 percent and 32 percent, respectively, of Soviet exports to the West by volume. The slight decline of imports in 1987 – parallel to a small increase in world prices – may support my previous findings.

A certain number of measures are currently being implemented to save energy, find substitutes for petrol, and reduce the ratio of energy consumption for every unit of income produced (the ratio is much higher than in any country in the West). These efforts, accompanied by modernized equipment, could well relieve the constraint on petrol, but would not automatically decrease re-exports. Intensively stepping up domestic production might not be on the agenda for the time being. Exploration and extraction costs have been growing for at least 10 years now. At present increases in oil production come mostly from West Siberia and other remote or deserted areas where major investments are needed. Soviet policymakers could find it cheaper to import oil from Middle Eastern and North African countries, especially while the terms of trade between civilian and military equipment, on one side, and petrol, on the other, continue to improve.

If oil prices remain slack, the USSR will likely maintain its high rate of imports (mostly on barter terms) to stabilize its convertible currency receipts as well as its shipments to CMEA partners and some developing countries. Moreover, Soviet arms sales policy will affect oil imports, because oil is the main repayment item that major petroleum producers can offer in times of financial constraint. Finally, it cannot be ruled out that oil re-exports might be spurred on by the present policy of accelerated industry modernization, which implies, in fact, a growing recourse to Western technologies (the USSR usually buys such technology in currencies other than the dollar). Dollar depreciation compounds the problem, because it undermines the purchasing power of Soviet oil revenues denominated in dollars.

Although a price taker on the oil market, the USSR has nevertheless pursued an active policy involving the three main sections of the world market in which it operates — the West, the CMEA countries, and the Third World. Third World imports have become a new feature of this policy.

The new attitude toward OPEC countries should be considered in this perspective. In 1985, the USSR established diplomatic relations with Oman and the UAE. In 1986, under a bilateral agreement involving oil production and trade, Kuwait offered expertise in developing offshore oil extraction for the USSR. At the same time, the two countries decided to service each other's oil markets, with Kuwait supplying the Asian and East African countries and the USSR delivering oil to European and North African partners. At the beginning of 1987, the USSR agreed to back OPEC export cuts by reducing its own to a certain extent. In April of the same year it agreed to charter three tankers to Kuwait after a series of Iranian attacks in the Persian Gulf.

Meanwhile, the USSR is trying to enlarge existing sources of supply. Countertrade cooperation agreements on prospecting for and producing oil have been signed with such friendly countries as Iraq, Syria, Angola, and South Yemen, while barter deals with Iraq and Iran have been recently concluded in exchange for military sales and refinery products respectively.

Soviet Imports of Third World Manufactures: A Boom Ahead?

Since the mid-1970s, the developing countries have demanded that the USSR increase the share of manufactured goods it imports from them. After a notable contraction during the 1970s, the USSR's share has steadily grown during the 1980s, reaching 18 percent in 1986 (table 7). The great majority of imports – 14 percent – is represented by the group "other manufactured goods," while machinery and equipment account for the rest. Both groups have shown a much larger than average increase in volume of imports.

These aggregate figures markedly conceal, however, different trends for individual commodity groups. Moreover, imports are heavily concentrated on a few groups and countries. An analysis of the market shares of some commodity groups indicates where trade specialization has taken place. "Textile yarn and fabrics" stands out as the strong sector of this trade. More than one-quarter of Soviet world imports of this group comes from the developing countries. Imports are extremely concentrated—28 percent of cotton fabrics come from India, with lower quantities coming from Pakistan (15 percent), Syria (16 percent), China (6 percent), and others. All together these imports constitute roughly three-quarters of Soviet world imports.

Almost all cotton yarn imported into the USSR comes from four Third World countries: Egypt (which supplies more than one-half), Vietnam, Syria, and Peru. More than one-third of wool fabrics are imported from India.

In many cases, such concentration results from various forms of cooperation, either through "conversion deals" or "product buy-backs." An example of a conversion deal with a nonsocialist country is the exchange of Soviet raw cotton for Indian textiles; in similar deals involving socialist countries, raw cotton is exchanged for Vietnamese, Chinese, and North Korean textile products. Imports of clothing have also grown through the years; the Third World share was 14 percent in 1986. Main suppliers are Pakistan, Syria, Yugoslavia, China, North Korea, and Vietnam.

Other goods are also imported—for example, Egyptian furniture and Indian medicines as well as various perfume and cosmetic products from the same two countries plus Syria. The developing countries' share of the "chemicals" group was roughly 9 percent in 1986.

Finally, Third World machinery and equipment account for a mere 1 percent of the Soviet market (7 percent if the socialist countries, namely Yugoslavia, are also considered). Here the bulk of nonsocialist imports are even more concentrated on India. In 1987 roughly 18 percent of Soviet imports from this Asian country consisted of this commodity group, including garage equipment, machine tools, pumps, auto parts, diesel engines, storage batteries, water-purifying plants, thermal units, lift trucks, and textile equipment. In a list prepared by Soviet organizations, Indian technologies and equipment of interest to the Soviet market range from the chemical sector to the metallurgical and the high-tech—for example, computer printers, plotters, memories, laser printers, and peripheral units.[11]

Some items may be produced under Western license or may be coproduced with Western firms. Of considerable importance are the two special Export Zones created in west India and near Bombay, respectively, where several Western multinationals have set up subsidiary plants to sell their products to the Soviet market. Besides chemical and cosmetic products, there is machinery, such as Rank Xerox photocopiers, assembled by the Indian firm Modi.[12]

In addition, Indian equipment is subcontracted to third countries in which the USSR is engaged in building industrial enterprises. Other countries are also beginning to sell some machinery and equipment to the USSR. Such products include Brazilian cables, computer components and platforms; Mexican pipes; Peruvian personal computers; Singaporean ships and platforms; and Turkish batteries. (Their values are for the moment very low, however.) Among the socialist countries, Yugoslavia stands out with a wide range of machinery and equipment representing 48 percent of its global exports to the USSR. But some Chinese bearings, automobile batteries, and hand tools are also sold to the USSR, as well as North Korean metal-cutting machines, electrochemical equipment, and batteries.

Barring a few exceptions like India, Soviet imports of nonsocialist Third World manufactures are still low, demonstrating until now this trade's secondary importance to Soviet policymakers. In 1987 only three of the top 10 Soviet partners had a share of all manufactures in their exports to the USSR of more than 20 percent: India—roughly 60 percent, and Syria and Egypt—about 70 percent. To these should be added four socialist developing countries: Yugoslavia—75 percent, North Korea—55 percent, Vietnam—38 percent, and China—25 percent. None of the well-established nonsocialist NICs are on the list.

The economic irrationality of this situation has pushed Soviet specialists to speak more and more openly about the possibility of a "redeployment" of some production lines from the USSR to the Third World.[13] This is viewed as part of a structural policy aimed at rationalizing international economic relations. Industrial consumer goods, the privileged object of this policy, is a sector in which the USSR is traditionally a net importer; such imports are mainly from Eastern Europe but also come from the West. Moreover, this relatively underdeveloped sector in the Soviet economy accounts for only 25 percent in total industrial production. Given the priority today for raising levels of consumption as an incentive to increase labor productivity, the prospect of higher imports seems all the more probable. The Third World is considered a possible source of such goods for two reasons. It enjoys a comparative advantage in their production, because it can offer them at much lower cost and does not suffer from the labor scarcity that has been plaguing the Soviet economy until now. At the same time it is finding Western markets extremely difficult to penetrate, because of growing protectionism in the West.

By "redeployment" Soviet specialists do not so much mean the relocation of some already existing labor-intensive production lines to the Third World, as has been the experience in the West. They point rather to the establishing of new production units there that are geared almost exclusively to the Soviet market.

There are now signs of such a structural policy in the gradually developing industrial cooperation – for example, the buy-back and conversion deals mentioned earlier. Straightforward imports have also increased. Many agreements in recent years include clauses providing for growth in the share of manufactures in Third World exports to the USSR. Typical agreements were the ones signed before the mid-1980s with Brazil and Bolivia, stipulating that Soviet foreign trade organizations spend all the revenue from their exports to these countries on purchasing goods from them, up to 30 percent in manufactures and semi-manufactures. Bartering is more recently used for this purpose, involving textiles from Uruguay and garments from Thailand and

Mexico. Another recent feature is for countries to repay debts to the USSR partially through industrial consumer goods. Algeria and Turkey use this method in exchange for credit lines received from the USSR. More important, Peru has started repaying an old military debt through exports of various manufactured products, such as footwear, textiles, clothing, and personal computers.

Soviet specialists increasingly consider it rational to purchase machinery and equipment from the most advanced developing countries. South Korea, Taiwan, Hong Kong, Brazil, Argentina, and Mexico, together with India, have even started to sell turnkey factories and to invest abroad through their own transnational companies. A wide range of sectors is involved, from the traditional metallurgical, chemical, and food industries to such industries as oil prospecting, civil engineering, construction, and various services. Many of these goods and services are bought by the West. Why should the Soviets not do the same?

In the medium term, there may be a surge of manufactured imports from the Third World. Whether this surge will imply a further rise in their share is an open question, depending on the other goods imported. If the terms of trade of manufactures continue favorably in relation to raw materials and commodities and the growing volume of raw materials and commodities does not offset the increase of manufactures, Soviet imports will be characterized by an increasing share of manufactured goods.

Soviet Machinery and Equipment: Breaking into the Southern Markets

Exports of civilian manufactures are creating problems for the Soviet Union. Apparently they have been a success in Third World markets. Their value has steadily increased, together with their nominal share in total identified exports to the developing countries, which rose to 54 percent in 1986 (38 percent is represented by "machinery and transport equipment"). But the rise in their share during the 1980s was entirely due to price increases, their volume growth, although positive, lagging behind average (table 7). These results are still better than the overall performance of Soviet machinery and equipment exports to the world at large. According to the head of the Statistical Section of the Soviet Ministry of Foreign Economic Relations, there was an average annual decrease of 0.5 percent in physical volume for 1981–1985 and of 1 percent for 1985–1987.[14]

The Third World still constitutes, however, an increasingly important outlet for Soviet products. In 1987, almost 47 percent of Soviet machinery and equipment exports were taken by this part of the world. Of this total, 22 percent was directed to the three CMEA partners, 5 percent to the other socialist countries, and 20 percent to the nonsocialist Third World.

During the 1980s, the Soviet share of the nonsocialist Third World's imports from the world has also grown; at 3.3 percent, however, it is still below its 1970 level of 4.7 percent. This minimal result was mainly due to economic and technical assistance programs. Roughly 80 percent of Soviet aid goes to industry and consists of industrial goods, not financial flows. On average, more than one-half of the machinery and transport equipment exported to the Third World has been delivered within the framework of projects built with the technical assistance of the USSR. This ratio in 1987 is higher than 70 percent for such countries as Mongolia, Vietnam, and Tunisia; it is higher than 80 percent for Bangladesh, Guinea, and Iran and is higher than 90 percent for the Congo, South Yemen, and Nigeria.

Not all of the remaining machinery exports are sold in normal commercial transactions. When these flows are not covered by the "clearing" umbrella, transactions have resorted to straight barter—for example, trolley-buses for Argentinian wine or Colombian coffee, tractors for Uruguayan butter or Mexican tubing strings, cars for Jamaican bauxite, helicopters for Guyanan bauxite, and metal-cutting machine tools for Brazilian instant coffee.

The USSR is increasingly tying the delivery of its machinery to the purchase of further quantities of commodities supplied by its structural creditors. Argentina, for example, has seen its new five-year grain agreement subordinated to the acceptance of Soviet equipment for hydroelectric plants.

From this perspective, results are rather disappointing. Something of a breakthrough of Soviet equipment into Third World markets had occurred in the 1960s. Soviet mass-produced equipment of an unsophisticated character, mostly in the basic industries, matched the growing demand arising from the industrialization programs in many developing countries. In the face of Western hostility, the only alternative for some of the newly independent nations was to approach the USSR. Moreover, the terms were rather advantageous, because they included long-term credits or barter arrangements. Foreign-exchange-starved countries could only look positively on these offers.

Since then, key sectors of heavy (mainly state) industry have received great impetus from Soviet assistance in various countries, with India in the lead. Steel and metallurgy, power generation, heavy electrical industry, coal mining, and onshore oil exploration are the fields in which Soviet technology is supposed to be on a par with the best in the world. The Indian Bhilai steel plant, the Aswan hydropower complex, the Euphrates Hydro-electric Power Station, and Syria's petrol industry are but a few of the many examples often quoted by Soviet sources as relative successes. Because Soviet equipment is sturdy, outdated, less sophisticated, and has built-in errors, it is sometimes thought to be more adapted than modern Western machinery to Third World conditions. An Indian expert recalls the debate that occurred in his country about West German and Soviet thermal generator sets. He argues that the marginally better thermal efficiency of the West German models loses its significance when, for other reasons, Indian capacity utilization remains much lower than the West's and transmission and distribution losses are about three times as high.[15]

In some other sectors also, Soviet products are beginning to be accepted. After visiting Soviet plants, delegations of Indian machine-tool industrialists have concluded that several of the Soviet machine tools are on a par with Western goods. From Latin America, Colombia has signaled positive experiences with Soviet tractors, trolleybuses, and textile machinery. But whatever their merits, Soviet equipment and technology transfer have aroused all sorts of complaints from the developing countries. Recently, Soviet specialists have joined the chorus as well.

A detailed study prepared by the Marga Institute of Sri Lanka on a tire and tube factory built with Soviet assistance in the 1970s offers an enlightening picture of some features of the Soviet transfer of capital goods.[16] The Sri Lankan experts showed that the capital cost of the project was high compared with similar projects set up by Western enterprises in neighboring countries. They then go on to list the reasons for this. Very often Soviet state enterprises are mostly interested in meeting their export targets and have a built-in tendency to promote investment on a larger scale than is required for the recipient economy. As a consequence, many of the plants carried unused capacity. There was also excessive expenditure on foreign personnel. Some of the equipment was bought abroad by the Soviet Union; direct purchase from the original source of supply by the Sri Lanka Tyre Corporation might have reduced the price. The cost was increased by the operational rigidity and inflexibility of the Soviet team in carrying out the project. And there was a tendency to overinvest in stocks of spare parts, because orders for spare parts sent to the main state firm had to be dispatched to the various producing firms. Finally, the price element was found to be a most elusive factor. Soviet agencies did not itemize the prices of each piece of equipment and obliged the Sri Lanka corporation to negotiate on the total price of the project.

Lacking product specifications, stocks of spare parts, and appropriate after-sales-services seem to be at the core of many other criticisms received since then from all over the globe. In addition, Soviet equipment is considered inadequate at times to operate under tropical climatic conditions. Soviet foreign trade organizations are also under fire for their unwillingness to deliver small sets for small-scale private enterprises. Poor presentation and marketing are cited as further obstacles. In some instances, the products from Soviet-assisted factories were difficult to sell on foreign and even domestic markets, as the Indians experienced with the Surgical Instruments Factory and the Drug Factory.[17]

Moreover, when it comes to expansion and modernization of the same units, the Third World often prefers Western partners. Such was the case, for example, of the three Indian engineering plants of Bharat Heavy Electricals Ltd. This was not an isolated case. French technology was preferred for an alumina plant, Italian know-how for a pharmaceutical company, and Japanese cooperation in the automobile industry. Western equipment is even installed in military goods. French navigational systems and air-to-air missiles are applied to Indian MiGs produced under Soviet licenses.[18] In the new Indian steel plant at Vishakhapatnam, the USSR provides only half of the capital equipment coming from abroad; the rest comes from the West.

Yet another factor endangers future prospects of Soviet sales. Some of the most advanced developing countries are themselves increasingly able to produce the basic industrial goods offered by the USSR, sometimes precisely because of previous Soviet assistance. One example is the different stages in the construction of Soviet-assisted Indian steel mills. The "domestic content" in the construction of Bhilai I was 15 percent; of Bhilai II, 70 percent; of Bhilai III, 85 percent; and of Bokaro I and II, 85 percent.[19]

Locally, these developing countries can produce complete sets of equipment and plants, which up to now have accounted for roughly 60 percent of Soviet exports of machinery and equipment. This intersectoral type of trade corresponded to a lower level of industrialization in those countries, but is inadequate at present, when they would prefer to set up their own machine-building industry. From this perspective, Soviet trade has not adapted yet to the new trend in the international division of labor, in which intra-industry trade prevails, with its flows of units, parts, and subsets for assembly.

The USSR is, in fact, suffering increasing competition from the more advanced developing countries, both in Western and in Third World markets.

On Western markets between 1980 and 1986, the Soviet Union suffered market share losses in all major commodity groups alike. This also includes the traditional Soviet success stories—namely, chemicals and passenger road vehicles, whose share of the Western market declined between 1980 and 1986 from 0.7 to 0.6 percent and from 0.8 to 0.2 percent, respectively. The figures for the developing countries are just the opposite: their market shares in the same two groups increased from 3.8 to 4.5 percent and from 0.6 to 2.2 percent, respectively. Globally, Soviet machinery and equipment declined from 0.3 to 0.1 percent of the Western market, while the Third World almost doubled its share (from 4.6 to 8 percent).[20]

Even on Third World markets, however, the USSR has not fared much better. In a recent study on competition between the developing countries and the East in Third World markets, I showed that, between 1980 and 1985, Asian developing countries, including China and some Middle Eastern countries, had larger increases in their market shares than the Soviet Union.[21] The path of export specialization followed by the USSR toward the South in the first half of the 1980s seems to counter its highly industrialized internal structure. During this period, the USSR has in fact increased the position of raw materials and intermediate products within its civilian exports to the South, while for its major competitors this ratio is declining. Also, geographically, the Soviet Union reveals a "bad" regional specialization, in the sense that it concentrates on regions or individual partners that show a lesser dynamism than the average. Such dynamic markets as South Korea and Taiwan are totally absent as an outlet for Soviet products, while Singapore and Hong Kong are still of minimal importance. The same results may be obtained by calculating the so-called export specialization indices. The index for Soviet machinery and equipment exports to the Third World shows a steady deterioration during the first five years of the 1980s, but it is improving for Third World competitors, except for Latin America.[22]

Several Soviet experts recognize by now that these difficulties cannot be wholly reduced to the Western-biased formation of Third World authorities and technicians, to political barriers, or to the lack of technical skills by local cadres.

Soviet journals have started to carry devastating criticisms. One article stated bluntly:

> The difficulty in developing Soviet exports of engineering products and finished products lies not so much in their non-competitiveness in price, as in the fact that these commodities are not fully up to the requirements of the world market as regards their technical standard, quality, finishing and other "nonprice" characteristics.[23]

Another well-placed specialist gives an interesting example of such inadequacy:

> Our industry has been turning out planes, motor vehicles, tractors, farm and road construction machinery having practically no differences from earlier models in terms of their specifications and exterior design. In particular, the main truck models are hopelessly outdated and do not meet the world market specifications as regards engine life. They are 25 and even more percent heavier than foreign analogues, often fail to meet the requirements regarding vibration and safety, and consume more fuel and lubricants.[24]

The failure to observe international technical standards has become a real obsession among Soviet authorities. There is reason to worry. According to the figures that circulated mostly in the scientific community in Moscow at the end of 1988, less than 30 percent of the products of the machine production industry, less than 14 percent of machine tools, and less than 17 percent of the products of the machine-tool construction industry are considered to be on a par with world standards. The causes of this state of affairs are increasingly attributed to the insufficiencies of the innovation sector and to the slow rate of renewal of equipment, most of which is reportedly more than 10 years old.

Various measures, announced recently, seem designed to improve the competitiveness of Soviet engineering products. At the end of January 1989, for example, the USSR signed an agreement with West Germany on industrial standards. And the state quality control introduced in 1987 was aimed at raising the quality and technical level of industrial products. A large portion of the enterprises and ministries that received the right to trade directly with foreign partners is in engineering. Engineering is also particularly privileged in the current five-year plan because of the investment funds devoted to it. The modernization of existing equipment is emphasized rather than new construction.

Will the new boost given to domestic production and the new international standards required for most of its products allow a real breakthrough in Third World markets? Paradoxically, the quest for efficiency and profits in convertible currencies seems to suggest that Soviet enterprises should avoid southern markets for the time being, because even richer developing countries are now plagued with balance of payments difficulties. It seems plausible, therefore, that Soviet machinery exports to the Third World would increase if the favorable credit terms of the past were enlarged rather than ended. More generous terms seem to be at odds, however, with Gorbachev's strategy.

Military Equipment Sales

Since the mid-1960s, military sales have occupied a large and increasingly important place in Soviet relations with the Third World. To arrive at a precise calculation of the value and quantity of this trade is an almost impossible task, given the secrecy surrounding such a matter (as is also the case in the West). There are two major ways of estimating Soviet arms sales. One is through mostly intelligence-based observations reproduced in documents from the Stockholm International Peace Research Institute (SIPRI), the Arms Control and Disarmament Agency (ACDA), the U.S. Department of State, and the Central Intelligence Agency (CIA). Such estimates are beyond the scope of this study and the author's capabilities. A second way — considering military sales as a function of the unexplained residues in Soviet exports to the Third World — calls for some qualifications.

The value of arms sales may be concealed in (1) the overall residue not identified by country of destination (as previously mentioned, presumably a minor part of it includes strategic materials and exports to other countries not reported in the Soviet foreign trade yearbook, while the rest — the majority — could well represent military equipment); (2) the intracountry residue — that is, the value of exports to the individual countries not identified by commodities; (3) the machinery and equipment subresidue — that is, the value of this commodity group not identified by individual items, when this is not already included under the previous heading; (4) the identified exports of machinery and transport equipment — for example, some of the aircraft and transport equipment (obviously the exact share of military sales under the previous three headings is mostly unknown);[25] and (5) deliveries that do not appear altogether in the yearbook. This is the contention of at least one Western analyst who argues that Soviet major weapons deliveries are not reported at all.[26]

In sum, one can only say that arms sales are certainly

larger than the overall residue. According to my own estimates, for example, in 1987 they were in the range of $9 billion, as opposed to $6.9 billion, of civilian exports to the nonsocialist Third World.

Whatever the absolute values, most Western analyses agree on the main trends in Soviet military sales of the past 20 years. In the mid-1970s and early 1980s, two large spurts occur, with a marked slowdown of their volumes after 1982–1983. Although it is certainly difficult to distinguish between politico-strategic and economic considerations, economic considerations have been playing an increasing role in this kind of trade. In fact, both periods of enhanced military sales follow the two oil shocks. Nearly 60 percent of these sales to the nonsocialist Third World are concentrated on four petroleum-exporting countries – Libya, Syria, Iraq, and Algeria. When petrodollars have been plentiful, these countries have been able (sometimes through such proxies as Saudi Arabia) to pay cash for increasing amounts of Soviet deliveries. Cash payments have been an economic motivation for the Soviet Union, because they relieve its hard-currency constraint.

No agreement exists among specialists about the exact contribution of military sales to the hard-currency trade balance of the USSR. Western estimates range from 15 to 60 percent in the 1970s and from 100 to 200 percent in the 1980s for the share of such sales in the nondefense hard-currency deficit. As will be discussed in the next chapter, Western figures are probably highly overestimated. It is nevertheless interesting that the volume sold has grossly followed the pattern of hard-currency revenues at the disposal of Soviet clients, decelerating after the first oil price decline in 1982–1983 and probably even more in 1986.

There are structural reasons why Soviet weapons could make such a breakthrough in Third World markets, even when payment in cash was required. Contrary to the average civilian equipment, Soviet military hardware appears to be competitive on world markets and well up to international standards. Rapid delivery and simplicity of maintenance add to its sale advantages. Defense in the USSR has been, until now, a top-priority sector that suffered almost no problems in the supply of intermediate goods or qualified personnel. Its built-in overproduction and the opportunity to reduce its unit production costs have been additional elements in the drive for exports.[27]

The situation in the late 1980s appears notably different, on both the demand and the supply side. Hard-currency receipts of oil-rich countries have been slashed, generally reducing imports, including military ones. The oil-rich countries increasingly demand concessionary terms, favorable long-term credits, or barter deals. Barter deals could be profitable for the USSR because they involve oil that could be re-exported to Western markets. The only country that seems to continue to receive increasing Soviet armaments is India. It receives roughly 15 to 20 percent of total Soviet military sales to the nonsocialist Third World, but repays its debts under a clearing scheme through which it delivers manufactured and primary goods. Competition is becoming harsher in what has become a buyer's market, where such aggressive newcomers as Brazil, South Korea, and Israel are developing military links with various Third World countries.

Even on the supply side, the situation has somewhat worsened. The production of military equipment requires resources that are more costly to extract each year, as well as an equipment supply that does not match domestic needs in the civilian economy. Moreover, the Western import content of these materials further increases their cost. Finally, the restructuring and modernization of the civilian economy should logically exacerbate the competition between the two sectors of the economy regarding claims on scarce resources and equipment.

Insofar as military sales are increasingly considered as exports, however, they will be treated as any other export. In this respect, the Soviet domestic defense cuts should have reduced the marginal cost of weapon exports, thus enhancing relative profitability.

It is impossible to forecast precisely the future evolution of Soviet military sales. Surely such sales will depend on the priority given either to politico-strategic imperatives or to the needs of the civilian economy.

5

Trade Balances and Payments Arrangements

The Trade Balance Triangle

A rather widespread thesis among scholars from all continents suggests that Soviet surpluses in convertible currencies with the South tend to compensate fully Soviet deficits with the West. (An earlier example in this volume involved arms exports.) This hypothesis raises quite a few important qualifications, however, about the way calculations are made on convertible currency receipts.

Data on Soviet overall trade balances with the nonsocialist Third World and with the West appear at first to support the thesis. In 1971–1981, the USSR had a $22.2 billion surplus with the developing countries as opposed to a $18.2 billion deficit with the West; in 1982–1987, the gap widened to a surplus of $32.4 billion and a deficit of $0.8 billion.

The Soviet deficit with the Western countries is in convertible currencies and can easily be checked against corresponding data from the West. But the picture is rather different as far as Soviet balances with the Third World are concerned. To ascertain the exact nature of these balances is a rather complicated procedure. The overall data reported in the Soviet foreign trade yearbook can be used to calculate an ascending trend for the overall Soviet surplus, which reached the considerable figure of $5 billion in 1987. The only slowdown occurred in 1985, when the surplus contracted to roughly $2 billion (table 9, first line). The result, however, of summing up all the balances with the identified developing countries is a constant and conspicuous negative balance, although it declined to $0.4 billion in 1987 in contrast to a peak of $2.5 billion in 1986 and 1985. What is left is a steadily rising surplus, not identified by countries, that reached more than $8 billion in 1987.

If the earlier discussion of the overall export residue is kept in mind, the most logical explanation is that the USSR achieves its surplus through shipments of military equipment and strategic materials; in the identified trade, however, which is mostly – but not all – civilian, it runs into deficits.[1]

This observation has to be qualified on two grounds. First the overall analysis has to be disaggregated into a regional and country-by-country study. Second, the meaning of these imbalances has to be examined in the light of the payments arrangements.

The regional breakdown of balances (table 9) shows that the USSR recorded a constant surplus in identified trade with Middle Eastern countries until 1983, with 1982 representing the peak ($2.1 billion). Since then, deficits of $200 million to $500 million have been occurring, except for 1986, which witnessed another small surplus of roughly $100 million. Considerable deficits with Iraq and Saudi Arabia (through 1986) are mostly responsible for such an evolution. As already suggested, these deficits might be connected with large shipments of oil to the USSR, which then re-exports it to the West.

Deficits with Africa mainly result from the deficit with Libya. Balances with Egypt, Sudan, Ghana, Guinea, and the Ivory Coast were also moderately negative in recent years. Soviet balances with Asia are greatly influenced by the balance with India. It was, in fact, the surplus obtained with India in 1983 (the first surplus since 1968) that re-

TABLE 9
Reported and Calculated Soviet Trade Balances with Nonsocialist Developing Countries, by Regions (exports minus imports in millions of foreign trade rubles and U.S. dollars)

Regions		1980	1981	1982	1983	1984	1985	1986	1987
Developing countries (reported total)	R	1,778	892	3,477	3,349	3,393	1,972	4,656	5,011
	$	2,740	1,240	4,788	4,508	4,161	2,355	6,610	7,914
Identified developing countries (calculated total)	R	−1,144	−2,488	−1,088	−1,597	−2,050	−2,131	−690	−259
	$	−1,877	−3,458	−1,498	−2,149	−2,513	−2,545	−979	−409
Africa	R	−141	−17	−445	−128	−507	−547	−673	−59
	$	−218	−24	−613	−173	−622	−654	−956	−93
North Africa	R	−137	−199	−832	−642	−903	−912	−802	−192
	$	−212	−277	−1,145	−865	−1,107	−1,090	−1,139	−303
Middle East	R	808	1,239	1,534	240	−414	−265	84	−105
	$	1,246	1,715	2,113	323	−507	−317	119	−166
Asia	R	−498	−798	−628	101	151	63	47	316
	$	−768	−1,110	−865	137	185	75	67	498
Latin America	R	−1,386	−2,911	−1,549	−1,810	−1,279	−1,381	−148	−410
	$	−2,137	−4,047	−2,133	−2,436	−1,568	−1,649	−210	−648
Net balance (not identified by countries)	R	2,922	3,300	4,565	4,946	5,443	4,103	5,346	5,270
	$	4,617	4,698	6,286	6,657	6,674	4,900	7,589	8,323

Note: The values in dollars have been converted from rubles at the official exchange rates.

Source: Calculated from *Vneshniaya Torgovlia SSSR v . . . g* (various years), and UN/ECE CPE (United Nations, Economic Commission for Europe, Centrally Planned Economies) Data Base.

versed the overall Soviet balance with Asia. During the period under review, the USSR maintained positive balances of trade in this region only with Afghanistan, Bangladesh, and Nepal. Soviet balances with all Latin American countries are traditionally negative, if Nicaragua is excluded.

In the 1980s, the Soviet Union has generally achieved a surplus with the three CMEA countries, the other socialist countries, and the socialist-oriented countries. The only exceptions are Cuba, with which it has had a deficit since 1985, China (since 1984), North Korea (until 1984), and Yugoslavia (in 1982 and since 1985).

Different Modes of Settlements

The significance of these balances would certainly be clearer if all payments were made in hard currencies. But this is not the case. From the beginning of its relations with Third World countries, the USSR established bilateral clearing accounts with many of them that allowed settlements in accounting dollars, sterling, or even (as in the case of India) in nonconvertible local currency (rupees). The advantages for both parties were obvious: they saved hard currencies, secured essential imports for their economies, while at the same time finding markets for their own products—that is, capital goods from the USSR and raw materials from the Third World. In an era of falling commodity prices, the developing countries found the long-term agreements with the USSR particularly attractive because they offered them, in principle, stability in prices as well as markets.

Along with the changes in the world economy of the early 1970s (rising prices for some primary products), there has been a growing tendency to include more and more convertible currency payments in mutual settlements. This multilateral method of payment was mainly requested by the Third World, but at the same time was welcomed by the USSR, which saw in it new possibilities of selling its manufactures for cash. The number of clearing agreements rapidly diminished from the 20 that existed in 1970. At present, the USSR has official bilateral clearing accounts with seven nonsocialist countries: Afghanistan, Bangladesh, Egypt, India, Iran, Pakistan, and Syria. In 1987 these countries accounted for 42 percent of the USSR's identified imports and 54 percent of its exports to the nonsocialist Third World. To these should be added the three CMEA countries, plus Yugoslavia, Kampuchea, and Laos, which also trade under a clearing umbrella.

A large part of Soviet trade with the developing countries then is still officially conducted through clearing agreements. But this is not the end of the story. Apart from the multilateral and the clearing mode of payments, the USSR also uses a third, mixed mode of payment. This method provides for payments in hard currencies for current export-import operations, while reverting to clearing for aid flows and repayments, plus some commercial transactions. Among the several nonsocialist countries that are supposed to trade under such a scheme, a Soviet source cites Cameroon, Chad, Congo, Nepal, Senegal, South Yemen, Sudan, Tanzania, Tunisia, and Uganda.[2]

Such a complex situation is bound to raise serious problems when calculations are attempted on the share of convertible currencies in this trade. Western analysts often suppose that all the developing countries without an official clearing agreement with the USSR settle their balances in hard currencies. Such is presumably also the way in which a Soviet author calculates that the share in 1983 of hard-currency trade has been mounting to 65 percent and 46 percent, respectively, for imports and exports to Third World countries.[3] In fact, this seems to be a rather arbitrary procedure.

The main issue is that a rigid distinction cannot be drawn between different settlement areas. First, the existence of clearing accounts does not preclude the conclusion of trade contracts in convertible currencies, as has been the case sometimes with Bangladesh and India. Second, trade not covered by clearing schemes may be only partially settled in convertible currencies. There may be compensation, barter and other kinds of arrangements in which credits and future repayments are made in kind. These have been particularly numerous in recent times, mostly because of balance of payments difficulties for many Third World countries. Third, the apparent surpluses should be further reduced by the value of Soviet machinery and equipment exported on long-term credits under the aegis of cooperation agreements. As mentioned earlier, on the average this volume includes more than one-half of all the machinery and equipment shipped to the Third World. Finally, in the cases of friendly countries or very poor developing countries, surpluses, whatever the mode of settlement, may not materialize at all, at least not for a long time. (The "bad" payers also include countries not covered by this category.)

Various factors contribute to the overall Soviet negative balance with the developing countries identified in the foreign trade yearbook. The Soviet Union has tended to run a surplus with the countries under clearing agreements (except for Egypt) and to run a deficit with the others. India is a special case. Until 1982, trade statistics showed a structural surplus with the USSR, but such an imbalance should not be taken at its face value. Some of it may be explained by Soviet inadequacy in meeting Indian advanced capital goods requirements, but most of it represents repayments for civilian and military credits received from the bigger partner.[4]

Further examination of the Third World by economic criteria reveals that the USSR tends to have a deficit with richer countries, with OPEC countries and NICs, while achieving a surplus with poorer countries. The surplus is likely to be higher with friendlier countries.

The problem remains as to how much of the export residue, mostly military sales, is settled in hard currencies. As Alan Smith has aptly pointed out, there is as yet insufficient evidence to indicate that the USSR actually received payments in hard currency for much of its arms deliveries in the 1970s.[5] This is true also in the 1980s. Since 1982, many oil-producing countries have pressed for oil-for-arms barter deals, with the balance presumably taking the form of long-term credits. The same reasoning can be developed for trade with the identified countries. Even surpluses denominated in a convertible currency may not be automatically and actually settled. An unknown part of it can simply be a Soviet credit in hard currency with the Third World. How much of these civilian and military credits will actually be repaid in the future is open to speculation.

As a result, the only plausible statement that can be made is that the Soviet surplus with the Third World may compensate only partially the deficit with the West. This has especially been the case of trade with North African and Middle Eastern countries, even when settlements were effected through barter. Southern oil could in fact be re-exported to the West for convertible currencies. There is evidence, however, that this "mini"-triangle of international payments is declining in importance not only for the USSR, but for the other East European countries as well.[6]

The question of modes of settlements, once a very heated subject in Soviet–Third World discussions, has now lost much of its impetus. Some debate still goes on in India, where critics of the clearing arrangement denounce the increasing dependence on Soviet supplies, the unfair rupee-ruble parity applied to long-term credit repayments, the price arrangements, and the excessive sheltering of Indian manufactures from international competition. As a result, some of them suggest going back to mutilateralism. Supporters of the present system point out that, although multilateral trade would eliminate short-term bottlenecks resulting from the accumulation of surpluses, it would likely lead to a contraction of trade and to a deficit. Moreover, the loss of the Soviet market for some of the Indian manufactured goods would not automatically convert into market gains in the West.

An overall Soviet reassessment of the function of the

clearing system may nevertheless be in the offing. According to a Soviet economist:

> The natural character of exchange is an overriding ele-
> ment of bilateral clearing agreements, since the choice
> and quantitative regulation of mutual shipments pre-
> cede the commercial contracts which fix the value pa-
> rameters of exchange. Such an order of things not only
> makes it difficult to maintain the value balance of bilat-
> eral exchange, but firmly establishes the administra-
> tive method of managing external economic relations,
> restricts the possibility of using the advantages of the
> international division of labour and maneuverability in
> winning new commodity markets, obstructs direct ties
> between Soviet enterprises and their partners abroad
> and hinders new forms of cooperation.[7]

Be that as it may, the question of imbalances is of growing concern, whether they are in clearing accounts or in
convertible currencies. Many developing countries that
have a persistent trade surplus with the USSR believe that
the surplus may cause a slowdown in reciprocal trade. This
issue is raised especially by partners adopting the convertible currency system. Argentina, Brazil, and various Asian
countries fear that their exports will stop increasing if the
present imbalance remains. The Third World countries at a
higher stage of development tend to have a surplus with the
USSR, while the opposite tends to be true of the less-developed ones. Here the problem lies mostly with Soviet exports. Even those Soviet goods that are fairly competitive
on the world market fail to find an adequate demand in the
above countries, as those countries tend to look to Western
markets for the more advanced equipment. On the contrary,
these same goods penetrate lesser-developed countries more
easily, provided that they are accompanied by financial arrangements to relieve the troubling foreign exchange gap.

One last word of caution should be mentioned here. The
Soviet Union does not publish balance of payments data.
Therefore, invisibles such as life insurance, freight, and in-

terest are out of the picture. In some instances, they might even reverse the visible trade balances, but unfortunately the lack of data makes it impossible to measure them.

Countertrade

Whatever the level of development and the official form of the payments system, in the 1980s the increasing debt burden and the depressed prices for their exports, coupled with limited access to international financing and growing protectionism on the Western markets, have pushed many developing countries along the road of increasing *countertrade* practices. According to a recent study, the reported countertrade deals involving developing countries rose from 18 in 1980 to a peak of 304 in 1985 and slightly diminished to 272 in 1987.[8] Although the authors adopt a rather broad definition of countertrade (including barter, buy-back, counter-purchase, bilateral trade and payments agreements, offset, debt for goods, and others), some of their findings are nevertheless relevant in our context.

East-South countertrade, although less important than North-South and South-South countertrade, accounts for more than 21 percent of all the developing country deals during 1980–1987. It is well above East-South share in world trade, which is about 3 percent. East-South countertrade increased more steadily over the period, reaching its peak in 1987. With 73 reported deals, the USSR has been by far the most active of the Eastern countries, accounting for one-quarter of the total. The USSR shows also the highest average value of deals in the world – roughly $600 million. Of the 56 reported "mega-deals" with a value in excess of $500 million, the East-South share involved 12 deals, 9 of which pertain to the USSR. The Soviet Union has signed more "mega-deals" with developing countries than any other single country in the world. The Third World countries involved are India with four deals, and Argentina, Brazil, China, Cuba, and Iraq with one deal each. In general, for all recorded Soviet deals, the leading partners are India and Brazil, with nine and seven deals respectively.

The economic motivations that have pushed the Soviet Union to rely increasingly on countertrade operations in most cases involved both exports and imports. Certainly the export promotion of its industrial products ranked high in importance, as did the strengthening of cooperation with some countries. At the same time, countertrade was used as a convenient tool to obtain raw materials, commodities, and in some cases manufactures. On the other hand, developing countries used it to market their surplus commodity exports or, in the case of India and some Latin American countries, to promote the export of their manufactured products. For both sides, the convenience of reducing foreign exchange disbursements has remained important.

Meanwhile, the developing countries are in a process of increasingly institutionalizing their countertrade practices, not only in Southeast Asia but also in Latin America and North Africa. In other countries, where similar institutions do not exist, countertrade regulations are being adopted to secure the same advantages of countertrade without incurring the losses frequently connected with it.

On the other side, the USSR might continue to respond positively to these countertrade offers from the developing countries. Soviet specialists insist that countertrade is one of the main avenues for expanding trade with the Third World. At present it represents a practice not only in intergovernmental agreements, but also in contracts signed by foreign trade organizations on purely commercial terms. In the USSR too, a process of institutionalization is under way. In 1988, the Bank of Foreign Economic Affairs, the State Bank, the Ministry of Foreign Economic Affairs, and other organizations jointly set up a new foreign trade organization named "Sovfintrade," especially tailored to carry out countertrade operations. At the same time, Soviet policymakers are taking pains to try to implement new forms of clearing agreements. One such proposal was made to the French "franc zone" countries to allow the transfer of balances with one country to the other countries of the zone. Similar offers have also been made to Latin American countries.

Will there be further impetus for this type of trade? If the financial situation of the developing countries remains unchanged, there will certainly be considerable pressures on them to travel this road. Countertrade is not the most efficient form of trade,[9] but until better international credit conditions are made available by the industrialized world, it might be one of the few ways left to the Third World to increase or at least stabilize its trade.

6

New Forms of Economic Cooperation

Soviet specialists increasingly refer to the so-called new forms of cooperation as ways to expand trade and deepen relations with developing countries. This all-encompassing term includes many different forms that distinguish it from straight trade or barter—for example, turnkey contracts, production-sharing arrangements, conversion deals, joint production, local assembly, subcontracting, trilateral cooperation, and joint ventures. In the West, many alternatives are known as "new forms of international investment"; others are rather classic forms of investment; and a few have a lot in common with countertrade. Nonetheless, all the phenomena described by the term are rather novel in Soviet practice or at least have undergone a significant quantitative increase in recent years. Sometimes two or more of these forms may be simultaneously involved.

Turnkey Contracts

Turnkey contracts appear to be one of the oldest of these new forms of cooperation. In such a deal, the Soviet contractor is fully responsible for setting up a complete project in the host country, whether in the productive or the infrastructural sphere. The Soviets supply feasibility studies, design and engineering, plant and equipment, specialists, training of local manpower, financing, and occasionally the construction of civic works. During the 1970s, Soviet turnkey contracts notably expanded, especially in petroleum-exporting countries and in some of the least developed countries. By the mid-1980s, the USSR had brought 150 turnkey projects to full operation in 18 developing countries, while 120 more were being implemented in various countries. By the same date, the share of turnkey projects in total Soviet assistance had risen to 47 percent, up from only 4 percent in 1970.[1] In some instances Soviet contractors subcontract portions of the works or may commit themselves to buying back the products of the project.

Production-Sharing and Buy-Back Arrangements

Production-sharing contracts or buy-back deals are no newer than turnkey contracts. They were developed by Western countries involved in the oil and mineral exploration of Third World deposits since the early 1960s, and the Soviets have replicated their use and enlarged their scope. Under this type of agreement, the USSR supplies equipment and technical assistance on credit to a developing country, which repays later through a predetermined share of the physical output from the unit that was set up with Soviet assistance. Sometimes such a deal is also called deferred compensation. The bauxite deposit at Kindia in Guinea provides a classic example. To repay costs of Soviet exploration, equipment, and technical assistance, 50 percent of the expected bauxite production for 30 years (beginning in 1975) would satisfy the initial credit; 40 percent would be exchanged against machinery, spare parts, and explosives; and 10 percent would remain at Guinea's disposal. More than 60 buy-back deals between the USSR and the developing countries exist today, ranging from oil (Iraq and Syria) to gas (Afghanistan), phosphates (Morocco), nitrogenous fertilizers (Afghanistan), pig iron (India), polymetallic ores

(Congo), tin concentrates (Laos), rare earth pegmatite and quartz (Madagascar), fluorspar (Mongolia), apatite (Vietnam), and natural rubber (Kampuchea and Vietnam). Although this form of cooperation has been mainly used to assure the USSR of a stable and long-term supply of certain kinds of fuels, mineral raw materials, and agricultural commodities, a few instances seem to indicate the expanding interests of the USSR. Rolled steel and metallurgical and hoist equipment appear to be included in deals with India; Chinese vegetables are jointly produced in northeastern China and delivered to the USSR in exchange for Soviet fertilizers and fuel used in their production. Vegetables and fruit are also the object of a deal with Vietnam. An alumina plant is being planned in India under a similar agreement, which has recently been extended to cover such manufactured items as light industrial goods from Vietnam and batteries and microelectric motors from North Korea. In Turkey, prospects are being considered for the joint construction of factories to produce car batteries, footwear, and cloth for jeans. At present one-half of Soviet imports from all the developing countries (including the socialist ones) are products turned out by Soviet-assisted enterprises. Only 10 years ago this share was one-quarter.

Conversion Deals

A variant of buy-back agreements, the so-called conversion deals, occur when the host country manufactures goods according to the orders and specifications of the Soviet Union, which supplies the necessary raw materials. Under such a contact, the Indian Council for Promotion of Wool and Wool Product Exports in Ludhi organizes mass production of knitted wool items, of which about 90 percent is being imported by the Soviet Union under a long-term commitment. Soviet wool is also sent to Vietnam, and finished textile products are imported from India, Vietnam, and North Korea against a supply of Soviet cotton. Medicaments are also involved in an agreement with Vietnam. In some cases (North Korea, for example), the USSR supplies not only the raw materials but also the necessary equipment and technical assistance. The USSR particularly benefits by developing such relations with neighboring countries that have large excess capacities to process Soviet raw materials produced in remote areas. Moreover, the lower labor costs and level of experience, as in the case of India, may offer the USSR considerable advantage in labor intensive production lines.

Coproduction

In the manufacturing sector, various coproduction schemes have also been developed for the joint production of special models of tractors in India, Pakistan, and Bolivia; transport equipment in Afghanistan; equipment for hydroelectric stations in Argentina; other heavy machinery in India; and watches in Panama and Hong Kong. It is not rare for a developing country to assemble finished products with the inputs provided by the Soviet Union. Contrary to the Western practice of selling the product either in the principal's market or in third country markets, the final products of Soviet cooperation have usually been sold in the host-country market and occasionally in third country markets. Some examples include the agreement to assemble MTZ-80/82 tractors in Ethiopia from units and parts supplied by the USSR; the long-term agreement on the assembly of Soviet tractors in Mexico; and the negotiations with Argentina, Brazil, and Ecuador to assemble Niva motorcars and farm machinery.

Joint Ventures

The most sweeping turnaround in Soviet official thinking has occurred in the area of joint ventures. A decree of January 13, 1987 allows, for the first time after World War II, the creation of joint ventures involving foreign capitalist partners, including developing countries, on Soviet territory. On September 17 of the same year, another decree officially sanctioned Soviet participation in joint ventures with developing countries on their territory.

Until that time, Soviet equity share ownership of enterprises established in the Third World occurred mostly in the trade and service sectors, with the notable exception of fishing. The exclusion, in principle only, of material production in countries with different socioeconomic systems was theoretically justified as follows: because they are nonproductive sectors, trade and services do not create any surplus value. The profit obtained by mixed firms in such fields does not stem from one partner's exploiting the other, but rather from the advantages of the international division of labor.

Be that as it may, the number of joint ventures was rather limited until 1988. The USSR does not publish balance-of-payments data to show its direct foreign investment. No agreement exists either in the Soviet Union or in the Western sources on the actual dimension of the phenomenon.[2] Research and interviews conducted by the author with Soviet scholars and authorities seem to indicate that there were a total of 30 joint ventures, wholly or partly owned by the USSR, operating in the Third World at the end of 1988. Because 5 of them belong to the CMEA developing countries (3 in Mongolia, 1 in Vietnam, and 1 in Yugoslavia) the total number for the nonsocialist Third World would amount to 25. Asia stands out as the preferred area of Soviet penetration with 44 percent of the ventures in the nonsocialist Third World. Africa is second with 9 mixed companies, the Middle East has 4, and Latin America has only 1. Location seems compatible with Soviet trade patterns only as far as Asia is concerned; the Middle East and Latin America are largely underrepresented. But a look at the individual countries where the ventures are set up causes even this slight consistency to disappear. Within Asia the ventures are concentrated in Afghanistan (4), Singapore (3), and Thailand (2) — not counting the 4 companies in Mongolia and Vietnam. India, the biggest nonsocialist commercial partner, until recently had only 1 such venture. In Africa, on the contrary, distribution is much more even; only Morocco has 2 companies, and the rest are spread over 7 countries. Here too, however, some of the major trade partners like Libya and Algeria are missing; in Nigeria, a joint venture failed for lack of profitability. The same occurs in the Middle East (Iraq, Syria, and Egypt are absent) and in Latin America (Peru is the only country represented).

Fisheries and transport seem to be the main sectors involved (9 joint ventures each); trading operations follow closely (7 companies). Three ventures concentrate their activities on prospecting for and developing natural resources in CMEA developing countries — namely, Mongolia (fluorspar, copper, and molybdenum) and Vietnam (oil).[3] Last come such sectors as banking and the assembling industry (1 company each).

On the whole, Soviet joint ventures in the Third World appear to be mainly set up to support foreign trade operations. Fisheries appear to be an exception more because some developing countries tied the presence of Soviet vessels to such a condition than because of an independent decision.

Such attitudes, as well as the geographical and sectoral pattern of Soviet joint ventures, are bound to change after the decrees are implemented. According to the India-USSR Chamber of Commerce and Industry, an agreement has been reached for 24 new joint ventures on Indian territory, mostly concentrated in the manufacturing sector. Of these, 10 are in the engineering branch, 6 in chemicals and pharmaceuticals, 5 in the food industry, 2 in ship repairs and maintenance, and 1 in consulting. Another 63 were proposed and received positive responses by September 1988.[4] Various other negotiations involve North Korean milling machinery, woodworking, and light industry; Kuwaiti oil; UAE trading; Egyptian assembly of Niva cars; Brazilian commercialization of vodka; Argentinian sales of Soviet anti-hail equipment; and Chinese paper processing, clothing, and furniture.

Are Soviet joint ventures in the Third World going to spread? There are certainly many obstacles. First, the financial constraint affects both the Soviet Union and the developing countries. One possible solution is for capital contributions to be in kind rather than in money. This is easier within clearing arrangements, as the case of India seems to point out. Another solution would be to transform existing Third World debts into equity shares. Peru seems to be open to such a possibility. Soviet specialists are actively studying this alternative also for Cuba, Mongolia, Vietnam, Mozambique, and Nigeria.

The new rights granted to Soviet enterprises to deal directly with foreign partners and their new regime of self-financing will make them very cautious about using foreign currency earned in export dealings. Profit motivation is likely to become a driving force, along with the more traditional support to trade operations.

Finally, a positive factor might be at work soon. Growing protectionism on the part of the developing countries could, paradoxically, motivate the Soviet Union to set up ventures inside those countries, just as the West does. Scarce foreign currency would be earmarked especially for such endeavors. Soviet companies still have a long way to go, however, in learning the entrepreneurial skills necessary for these operations. Soviet journals are beginning to discuss a new form of investment cooperation—namely, the BOT (build, operate, transfer). Under such a scheme, the foreign partner of the joint venture is fully responsible for the effective operation of the project during the period of time (10 to 15 years) necessary to recoup the expenses. After that date, the management of the project is transferred to the host partner, who will have acquired the necessary experience. Favorable opportunities for Soviet organizations are seen in the construction of big capital-intensive projects, such as power stations, railways, motorways, and sea and air terminals. One such scheme, an energy project, is currently being planned in Turkey.[5]

As mentioned previously, the motivations behind the new decrees allowing joint ventures on Soviet territory are the acquisition of top technology and management, hard-currency receipts from exports on Western markets, and domestic production that can substitute for imports. The initial reaction that this might rule out capital-deficient developing countries would be too rash. Services stand out as one possible sector of cooperation, while NICs could become active partners in the technology sectors or even in the development of Soviet mineral resources.

According to the Soviet Ministry of Finance, by February 15, 1989, there were already 258 registered joint ventures: 204 with the West, 25 with Eastern Europe, and 29 with the Third World. Among the ventures with the Third World, 9 involve the socialist developing countries. Yugoslavia is the leader with 6 ventures, which range from the production of turbines, programmed controllers, and plastic products, to consulting and engineering services. The other 3 are with North Korea (pulse-wave technology and miscellaneous consumer goods) and China (catering services). Of the remaining 20 joint ventures, India leads the way with 5 joint ventures (catering, computers, miscellaneous consumer goods, publishing, tourism); Brazil has 3 ventures (textiles, miscellaneous consumer goods and services); and Singapore (personal computers, sea products), Syria (medical services, publishing), Kuwait (engineering services, catering), and Cyprus (perlite products) have two ventures each. The rest involve Panama (business services), United Arab Emirates (transport machine building), Venezuela (publishing), and Iran (business services).

New joint ventures are under way: the Indians want to establish another restaurant in Tashkent and to invest in a Siberian paper and pulp plant. The opening of a Turkish restaurant in Moscow is being discussed. The Brazilians, in conjunction with a Swedish company, have signed a technical protocol for setting up a fruit juice factory. Establishing joint state farms for growing vegetables and soybeans is also being discussed with North Korea.

Aside from the lack of capital, obstacles to forming joint ventures with developing countries on Soviet territory appear very similar to those the West has in this regard: the inconvertibility of the ruble, the difficulty of evaluating the partner's equity shares, the unreliability of supplies inside the USSR, and problems related to investment protection, prices of Soviet inputs, and guarantees from Soviet banks. It is an open question how many of the initial joint ventures set up on Soviet territory are going to be simply a cover for such older types of cooperation as compensation agreements.

Third Markets

Soviet authorities seem to be renewing their interest in cooperation in third markets. In fact, joint ventures abroad sometimes result from previous cooperation in third markets. The economic motivations for such operations – including expansion of the potential market, access to new markets, diversification of sources of supply, convertible currency earnings, and strategic geographic location – are well known in the West. For the Soviet Union, this cooperation can involve either developing countries alone or also the Western developed nations.

The USSR tends to cooperate in third markets mainly with those developing countries that possess a diversified and relatively more advanced economic structure; well-established bilateral cooperation ties and specific expertise are additional favorable factors. Indian firms emerge as natural candidates, very often as subcontractors for Soviet prime contractors in the Third World. Indian-made equipment has been supplied to Soviet organizations engaged in building steel mills (Nigeria, Iran, and Turkey), metal works (Algeria), aluminum works (Yugoslavia), nuclear power works (Libya), and nickel works (Cuba). NICs also are beginning to be sought. Construtora N. Odebrecht from Brazil participates with equipment and engineering for the Capanda Dam project in Angola. Another Brazilian firm, Furnas, supplies technical assistance, and the Soviet Union supplies turbines and generators. Turkish construction companies with extensive experience in North Africa and the Middle East, may contribute to the joint construction of the M'Jara hydropower station in Morocco.

Tripartite Industrial Cooperation

In the most classic form of tripartite industrial cooperation (TIC), a Western partner provides advanced technology, the USSR provides intermediate equipment, and the recipient developing country contributes public works, labor, and other resources. In cases where the recipient has a highly developed subcontracting activity, several structural components are provided by local firms.

A typical example is demonstrated by the operations of the United Power Corporation (UPCO) in Third World thermal projects, a simple joint venture established between the Finnish firm Kontram and the Soviet organization Technopromexport. When operational, the Soviets supply the complete turbogenerator set and in some cases the switchgear and transformers too; the remaining more sophisticated equipment (control systems and the like) are supplied by Finnish (or other Western) manufacturers; finally, public works are carried out by a local firm.[6]

The technology gap between the West and the Soviet Union lies at the very root of many TIC operations. Since the end of World War II, experience seems to indicate that the most appropriate technology for developing countries is not the most advanced on the markets. In fact, very often it proves to be a combination of Western and Eastern equipment and technological processes. This is especially true for energy projects. Soviet enterprises can easily supply standard large-scale equipment (that is, turbine-generator sets) on short notice, but they are rarely able to provide either critical equipment and components required by these standard items (exciters, control systems, and such), or more advanced technologies (for example, steam generation technology); such technologies are then subcontracted to Western manufacturers. This is also the experience of the Swedish firm ASEA in cooperating with the USSR on Latin American and North African markets.[7]

An interesting analysis of 255 TIC cases involving all the Eastern countries for the period 1958–1981 seems to confirm the division of labor discussed earlier.[8] TIC consists of a combination of tasks that can be ranked by the degree of skills required—mechanical engineering, subcontracting of equipment, assembly, and civil engineering. From this point of view, TIC seems to reflect accurately the relative position of the three partners on the world technological ladder: The West concentrates almost entirely on engineering and equipment; the East is much more specialized in equipment, but participates also in mechanical engineering, assembly and/or civil engineering; while the South sees its work structure dominated by civil engineering, with a slight contribution to equipment.

Soviet participation in this type of industrial cooperation is rather diversified and covers most of the industries except machine tools. In 1985, construction and various services (tourism and hotel management, for example) were roughly 33 percent of the total; metallurgy (including mining) was 20 percent, mechanical engineering 17 percent, the chemical industry 10 percent, and transport equipment 7 percent; other sectors accounted for 3 percent each.

The Soviet Union is rather keen on TIC operations for several reasons, two of which are often quoted by Soviet specialists. First, TIC effectively expands the export of Soviet machinery and equipment, some of which could not even be sold without Western cooperation. Second, it is a way to balance the deficits with Western countries through countertrade arrangements.[10] Other advantages should not be underestimated, however. In several instances, the products of the factory can be sold on Western markets for convertible currencies. The currencies could also be obtained as a form of financing through World Bank project funding, which obviously would not apply to the Soviet Union alone. Moreover, the USSR might acquire some of the advanced technology used in the process. And finally, TIC might be a way to balance structural trade deficits with several developing countries.

Equally positive motivations can be found for the other partners. Most of the reasons for the USSR are also valid for Western firms. Soviet participation allows the Western firms to lower the total cost of the operation and so to win international bids. And the South can obtain production units it could not otherwise afford and participate in the projects by performing the lowest level tasks. All of this explains why TIC has grown rapidly through the years. Until the mid-1980s, it was one of the most dynamic forms of Soviet-Western trade. The share of TIC contracts related to the total number of Soviet industrial cooperation contracts with the West has grown from 5.1 percent in 1981 to 8.2 percent in 1985.[11] More than 45 developing and 25 Western countries were said to be involved in the deals. A Soviet source mentions more than 300 examples of TIC, most of them in the developing countries.[12] Since 1985, progress has slowed down somewhat, especially in large-scale industrial projects. Declining oil revenues, increasing debt burden, high interest rates, global tensions, and the unwillingness of bankers to grant financing were certainly at the root of the problem. As some of these factors subside or disappear, this form of cooperation may witness a new upsurge.

7

In Search of Strategy:
Obstacles and Prospects

In my attempt to outline what appears to be a new Soviet strategy toward the Third World, three main trends in Soviet attitudes have emerged. (1) The USSR is not willing to abandon its three CMEA partners, although it insistently urges them to restructure their economies, partly because of the growing needs of the Soviet domestic economy. Some of the Soviet burden in providing assistance would then be recouped through more profitable trade ties. (2) On the other side, the friendly socialist-oriented countries appear to be left more to their own devices than they used to be and are pressed to look for additional assistance from other sources. With both types of countries the USSR could begin to have a much less generous attitude toward structural trade surpluses, which do not materialize either into convertible currencies or for that matter even into future goods deliveries, but only mean a net transfer of Soviet resources. Balances with Cuba have already started showing deficits in some recent years. These imbalances are not due to increased price subsidies for Cuban sugar, because sugar's unit value contracted by 11 percent in 1986 and 2 percent again in 1987, while the quantities declined as well in 1987. (3) The USSR seems more inclined to look for relatively advanced and potentially wealthier partners, such as

Brazil and South Korea, as well as the oil-rich states among the other developing countries.

No Room for Euphoria

The introduction of self-financing, the right to trade directly with foreign partners, and the right to retain a share of the convertible currencies earned do not mean an automatic increase in activity between enterprises, because some Third World countries might prefer safer state relations. In addition, the partial decentralization of the Soviet foreign trade monopoly could produce more difficulties for the developing countries in the short run. From now on, they will actually have to approach hundreds of enterprises instead of one or two foreign trade organizations. The Soviet market is bound to become more exacting, which will require larger efforts in marketing and sales promotion.

The obstacles to expanding Soviet–Third World economic relations are still formidable. Until the reform of the Soviet price system is implemented, Soviet enterprises will not be able to calculate exactly the profitability of the export-import mix. Lack of ruble convertibility adds to these problems. The preference of Soviet organizations for big state deals dies hard, while the developing countries are often interested in small-scale, private business.

The quality, the technological complexity, and the marketing of many Soviet industrial products is not yet on a par with similar Western items; the domestic supply of the NICs and of the second generation of manufactures exporters has been enhanced so as to require more sophisticated and advanced goods. These countries are actual or potential competitors with the USSR on the world markets. The built-in defects of bilateral trade and payments agreements, which account for a large part of Soviet trade with the Third World, is an additional constraining factor. India is the only outstanding case in which the clearing system does not appear to be a straightjacket, although much of mutual trade is spurred by Soviet military sales repaid in Indian civilian goods. Last, but not least, Soviet–Third World trade is seen in most official circles in the USSR as secondary to Soviet economic relations with the West.

All of these elements leave no room for euphoria in the short and medium term. Paradoxically, for the time being, the general lack of hard currency, depressed commodity prices, and growing Western protectionism might provide a miraculous mix to keep alive civilian trade flows and sustain the military ones somewhat as well. The developing countries, pushed by hard necessity and by the will to diversify their trade patterns, might opt for the USSR as an alternative partner, under all kinds of countertrade agreements. These agreements, however positive they may be for Third World commodities in search of an outlet, would compound the negative aspects of both systems as far as manufactured goods are concerned. Sheltered in the niches of various forms of compensation deals, the developing countries' manufactures would be isolated from international competition and risk a gradual lowering of their relative technological level.

In the longer term, prospects appear to be uncertain. On the one hand, the economy of the less-industrialized developing countries is still complementary to the Soviet economy. Soviet internal reforms could make available larger volumes and better quality industrial goods, and raw materials and consumer goods will be increasingly required by the expanding Soviet economy. Soviet exports to the Third World, although still dominated by manufactured goods, might witness a diminishing ratio between military and civilian sales. The import value of industrial consumer goods should substantially rise. More room should be occupied by intra-industry specialization, both with NICs and with lesser-developed countries, reducing the place of the present regressive interbranch specialization. Services should make their forceful appearance on the scene, ranging from construction works to engineering consulting and from tourism to transport and financial services.

Soviet Interest in International Economic Organizations

On the other hand, eventual Soviet participation in such international multilateral organizations as the IMF, the World Bank, or the GATT might entail new conflicts of interests with the Third World. Recent Soviet approaches to the GATT have received considerable attention in the West. On August 15, 1986, the USSR formally requested the GATT to take part as an observer in the Punta del Este international trade negotiations. The request was rejected mainly on the grounds that the GATT principles refer to decentralized market economies.

According to such strict principles, the restructuring under way in the USSR under Gorbachev cannot yet be defined as the creation of a market economy. As for the external sector of the economy, the decentralization of the foreign trade monopoly is not complete; some strategic materials are still being handled by specialized foreign trade organizations under the aegis of the Ministry of Foreign Economic Relations.

Because of the inconvertibility of the ruble, there still is no automatic connection between domestic and world prices. Applying differentiated currency coefficients could be considered as a form of export subsidy and of a nontariff restriction on imports. Moreover, the USSR does not have a customs tariff system; if and when it does have one, it would still not be able to negotiate on it because the tariff is meaningless while the foreign trade monopoly is still present (even if only partially present). As some highly placed Soviet officials have recognized, at least two years are needed for the Soviet Union to begin to reform its domestic price structure and then to change its external tariffs. Full external ruble convertibility is not finally expected before the end of the century.

Nevertheless, these rigid criteria were not applied by the GATT to other CMEA countries—Czechoslovakia (an original member), Romania, Poland, Hungary, and Cuba are full members, while Bulgaria is an observer to the GATT. Each one of them was subject to different conditions for participation. Another socialist country, China, is also about to resume its membership. A pragmatic solution regarding the USSR would thus be more in line with the tradition of the GATT's relations with state trading economies, although it would be pertinent to reassess the state trading countries' participation in the GATT.

What drives the Soviet Union to seek some form of association with the GATT? What benefits might it expect as a result, and what possible impact might its participation have on its relations with the Third World countries?

Although the Soviet approach to international multilateral organizations should be seen in light of Gorbachev's new outlook on foreign relations at large, there is a more precise economic rationale for the USSR's renewed interest in the GATT in the 1980s. Since 1982-1983 (and especially in 1986), the world has experienced a sharp decline in energy prices that has dramatically reduced Soviet convertible currency export receipts on the Western markets. As a result, trade officials have stressed the need to sell more manufactured goods to the West as a way of subtracting its receipts from the vagaries of the world commodity market.

What are the benefits the USSR might receive from eventual membership in an organization that focuses mainly on trade in manufactures? The expanded export of Soviet manufactures to the West could be expected, as well as possible acquisition of most-favored-nation (MFN) status (the same favorable treatment reserved for any other contracting party of the GATT). In its relations with some West European partners, the USSR already benefits de facto from a partial MFN clause that covers only tariffs; under the GATT the clause would include quantitative restrictions also. Negotiations are under way in the GATT on agriculture and services, which interest the USSR as an importer in the case of agriculture and as both an importer (in high technology) and an exporter (in maritime transport, etc.) in the case of services. But eventual participation in the GATT could further stimulate internal reforms in the Soviet economy.

How might Soviet membership in international organizations affect its relations with the developing countries? First, taking part in multilateral organizations such as the GATT (and the IMF and the IBRD) might entail some changes in the predominantly bilateral mode of Soviet international settlement with the Third World, particularly in the area of clearing. Second, the lowering of Western protection on some Soviet industrial exports might make them more competitive in Western markets, especially if the industrialized members of the GATT were to stop placing the NICs (which are among the USSR's harshest competitors) in a privileged status as developing economies—a status that entitles them to more favorable conditions under the General System of Preferences (GSP) scheme. Finally, other possible conflicts may arise with the interests of the developing countries in trade in services, a field in which the USSR would stand, for its own reasons, side by side with Western multinationals for the elimination of all restrictions.

In conclusion, the Soviet Union is moving away, albeit slowly, from its traditional "vent for surplus" approach to foreign trade, when excess production was intended for export in order to acquire imports that could not be produced at home. In the area of both exports and imports, there is a new, more cost-conscious attitude somewhat resembling (although, because of artificial prices and inconvertible currency, it cannot yet be the same as) the well-known comparative advantage approach. New areas of competition are bound to appear in the future with the developing countries, as well as with the West. At that point, the Soviet Union should begin to receive the same consideration as any other partner in the international economy. Trade conflicts might then replace political or military confrontations, just as they do in the Western community.

Notes

Chapter 1

1. I. D. Ivanov, "The Soviet Union in a Changing Global Economic Setting: The Prospects for Trade-Oriented Growth," Geneva, UNCTAD/ST/TSC/4, April 25, 1986, p. 6.

2. M. S. Gorbachev, "Politichesky doklad Tsentral'nogo komiteta KPSS XXVII S'ezdu Kommunisticheskoi Partii Sovetskogo Soyuza," *Kommunist*, no. 4 (1986): 19.

3. Francis Fukuyama, "Gorbachev and the Third World," *Foreign Affairs* (Spring 1986): 715–731; Francis Fukuyama, "Patterns of Soviet Third World Policy," *Problems of Communism* (September/October 1987): 1–13.

4. Elizabeth Kridl Valkeiner, "The USSR and the Third World: Economic Dilemmas," in *Soviet Foreign Policy in a Changing World*, R. F. Laird and E. P. Hoffman, eds. (New York: Aldina, 1986), 731–757; idem, "Revolutionary Change in the Third World: Recent Soviet Assessments," *World Politics* 38, no. 3 (April 1986): 415–434; idem, "New Soviet Thinking about the Third World," *World Policy Journal* (Fall 1987): 651–674.

5. "Programma Kommunisticheskoi Partii Sovetskogo Soyuza: Novaya redaktsiya," *Pravda*, March 7, 1986, p. 7.

6. Peter Wiles, ed., *The New Communist Third World* (London: Croom Helm, 1982), 364.

7. *Sotsialisticheskaya orientatsiya osvobodivshikhsia stran. Nekotorye voprosy teorii i praktiki* [Socialist orientation in the

101

liberated countries. Some problems of theory and practice] (Moscow: Mysl, 1982), 33–179.

8. Roger E. Kanet, "The Soviet Union and the Third World from Khrushchev to Gorbachev: The Place of the Third World in Evolving Soviet Global Strategy," in *The Soviet Union, Eastern Europe and the Third World*, Roger E. Kanet, ed. (Cambridge, England: Cambridge University Press, 1987), 3–22; Daniel Pineye, "The Bases of Soviet Power in the Third World," *World Development* 11, no. 12 (December 1983): 1083–1095.

9. Marie Lavigne, "Soviet Trade with LDC's," in *Gorbachev's Economic Plans*, vol. 2, Study Papers submitted to the U.S. Congress, Joint Economic Committee (Washington, D.C.: U.S. Government Printing Office, November 1987), 504–531.

10. Quoted from "Programma Kommunisticheskoi Partii," 7.

11. Karen Brutents, "Introduction," in *Co-operation between the USSR and Developing Countries* (Moscow: USSR Academy of Sciences, Institute of Oriental Studies, "Social Sciences Today" Editorial Board, 1986), 9.

12. *Tipologiya nesotsialisticheskikh stran (opyt mnogomernogo statisticheskogo analiza narodnykh khoziaistv)* [Typology of the nonsocialist countries: An attempt at multidimensional statistical analysis of the national economies] (Moscow: Nauka, 1976).

13. A. Ya. Elyanov and V. L. Sheinis, eds., *Razvivayuschiesia strany: ekonomicheskii rost i sotsial'nyi progress* [The developing nations: Economic growth and social progress] (Moscow: Nauka, 1983); Anatoly Elyanov and Victor Sheinis, *Developing Nations at the Turn of the Millennium* (Moscow: Progress Publishers, 1987).

14. Ibid., 45.

15. Elizabeth Kridl Valkeiner, *The Soviet Union and the Third World: An Economic Bind* (New York: Praeger, 1983); Thomas J. Zamostny, "Moscow and the Third World: Recent Trends in Soviet Thinking," *Soviet Studies* 36, no. 2 (April 1984): 223–235. An interesting analysis of 21 developing countries' having tried to apply the Soviet industrialization model can be found in Wladimir Andreff, "Le modèle d'industrialisation sovietique: Quelles leçons pour le Tiers Monde?" *Revue Tiers Monde* 28, no. 110 (April–June 1987), 263–285.

16. Elyanov and Sheinis, *Developing Nations*, 305.

17. Barbara Zochowska-Despiney, "Les pays socialistes face

au Nouvel Ordre Economique International," Thèse de 3ᵉ cycle, Université de Paris I, 1982.

18. "Declaration on the Restructuring of International Economic Relations," *Foreign Trade, USSR*, no. 12 (1976): 2–5.

19. UNCTAD, "Evaluation of the World Trade and Economic Situation and Consideration of Issues, Policies and Appropriate Measures to Facilitate Structural Changes in the International Economy," document presented by the CMEA countries to the 5th session of UNCTAD, Geneva, TD/249, April 19, 1979.

20. E. E. Obminsky, "Ekonomicheskii rost v razvivayushchikhsia stranakh i mirovoe kapitalisticheskoe khoziaistvo" [Economic growth in developing countries and the world capitalist economy], in *Razvivayushchiesia strany vo vsemirnom khoziaistve* [The developing countries in the world economy] (Moscow: USSR Academy of Sciences, Institute of World Economy and International Relations, 1987), 95–117.

21. O. Bogomolov, ed. *Sotsializm i perestroika mezhdunarodnykh ekonomicheskikh otnoshenii* [Socialism and the restructuring of international economic relations] (Moscow: Mezhdunarodnye otnosheniya, 1982).

22. Elyanov and Sheinis, *Developing Nations*, 178–179.

23. Igor Artemiev and Fred Halliday, *International Economic Security: Soviet and British Approaches*, Discussion Paper No. 7 (London: Royal Institute of International Affairs, 1988).

24. UNCTAD, "Assessment and Proposals by the Group of 77 Relating to UNCTAD VII," Note by the Secretary-General of UNCTAD, Geneva, TD/330, May 7, 1987, pp. 33–34.

25. UNCTAD, "Approach of the Socialist Countries Members of Group D and Mongolia to the Substantive Items of the Provisional agenda for UNCTAD VII," Geneva, TD/333, June 5, 1987, p. 12.

Chapter 2

1. "Economic and Financial Co-operation of the Union of Soviet Socialist Republics with Developing Countries," Note by the UNCTAD secretariat. Document presented to the 35th session of the UN Trade and Development Board in Geneva on September 19, 1988, TD/B/1191, September 23, 1988, p. 3.

2. Quintin V. S. Bach, "A Note on Soviet Statistics on Their

Economic Aid," *Soviet Studies* 37, no. 2 (April 1985): 269–275; Quintin Bach, *Soviet Economic Assistance to the Less Developed Countries: A Statistical Analysis* (Oxford: Clarendon Press, 1987), x-xxi; Marie Lavigne, ed., *Les relations Est-Sud dans l' économie mondiale* (Paris: Economica, 1986), 119–127.

3. Percentages were calculated from information found in *Development Co-operation, 1988 Report* (Paris: Organization for Economic Co-operation and Development, December 1988).

4. Hari Bhushan, "Role of Aid and Technology Transfer: Performance and Prospects," in *Indo-CMEA Economic Relations*, Suresh Kumar, ed. (New Delhi: Ashish Publishing House, 1987), 190.

5. "Economic and Financial Co-operation," 4.

6. *Narodnoye Khoziaistvo SSSR v 1985, 1986, 1987 g* [National economy of the USSR in 1985, 1986, 1987] (Moscow: Finansi i statistika, 1985, 1986, 1987).

7. Igor Ushkalov and Boris Heifets, "For More Effective Assistance," *Foreign Trade, USSR*, no. 10 (1988): 8.

8. Alexander Yampolsky, "USSR-Vietnam: Improvement of Trade and Economic Ties," *Foreign Trade, USSR*, no. 5 (1988): 7.

9. Giovanni Graziani, "The Non-European Members of Comecon: A Model for Developing Countries?" in R. E. Kanet, ed., *The Soviet Union, Eastern Europe and the Third World*, 163–179.

Chapter 3

1. Barry L. Kostinski, *Description and Analysis of Soviet Foreign Trade Statistics*, Foreign Economic Reports No. 5 (Washington, D.C.: U.S. Department of Commerce, July 1974); Giovanni Graziani, "Commercial Relations between Developing Countries and the USSR: Recent Trends and Problems," Paper presented to the first annual scientific meeting of AISSEC, the Italian Association for the Study of Comparative Economic Systems, Turin, Italy, October 25–26, 1984; Giovanni Graziani, "Soviet Strategy in Restructuring Trade with the Third World," in *The Soviet Economy: A New Course?* R. Weichhardt, ed. (Brussels: NATO Economics Directorate, 1987), 289–314; Laure Després, "Les ventes d'armes de l'URSS et des six pays socialistes européens aux pays en voie de développement," in *Les relations Est-Sud dans l'économie mondiale*, Marie Lavigne, ed., 57–73.

2. Anita Tiraspolski, "Les relations économiques de l'URSS et de l'Europe de l'Est avec les pays observateurs au CAEM," *Le Courrier des Pays de l'Est*, no. 314 (January 1987), 3–42.

3. *Pravda*, September 18, 1988.

4. *Financial Times*, December 15, 1988, and January 9, 1989.

Chapter 4

1. Graziani, "Commercial Relations between Developing Countries and the USSR"; Deepak Nayyar, "East-South Trade," in *Theory and Reality in Development*, Sanjaya Lall and Frances Stewart, eds. (London: Macmillan, 1986), 240–269.

2. Graziani, "The Non-European Members of Comecon," 163–179.

3. *Pravda*, October 14, 1988.

4. *Izvestiya*, October 14, 1988.

5. *Pravda*, November 4, 1988.

6. Thomas A. Wolf, "An Empirical Analysis of Soviet Economic Relations with Developing Countries," *Soviet Economy* 1 (July–September 1985): 232–260; Giovanni Graziani, "Soviet Prices in Trade with the Third World," Paper presented to the third AISSEC meeting, Siena, Italy, October 17–18, 1986; and idem, "Influence and Policy Implications of the Major Factors in Inter-Systems Trade, Especially in East-South Trade," Study prepared for the UNCTAD Secretariat, Geneva, August 1989.

7. Richard Levine, "Soviet Union," *Mining Annual Review* (London), published by the *Mining Journal* (June 1988): 435–445.

8. Graziani, "Soviet Strategy in Restructuring Trade," 296–297. See also, Sonia Bahri, "Les relations économiques entre les pays socialistes européens et les pays de l'OPEP," in *Les relations Est-Sud dans l'économie mondiale*, Marie Lavigne, ed., 171–203.

9. Giovanni Graziani, "Energy in Soviet-West European Relations," in *Pétrole: Marchés et stratégies*, A. Ayoub and J. Percebois, eds. (Paris: Economica, 1987), 302–320.

10. Giovanni Graziani, *Comecon, domination et dépendances* (Paris: Maspero, 1982); Giovanni Graziani, "La dépendance énergétique de l'Europe Orientale vis-à-vis de l'URSS: 1945–1982," *Revue d'Études Comparatives Est-Ouest* 14, no. 2 (June 1983): 37–60; Giovanni Graziani, "Capital Movements within the

CMEA," *Soviet and East European Foreign Trade* 22, no. 1 (Spring 1986): 19–50.

11. India-USSR Chamber of Commerce and Industry (IUCCI), *IUCCI Newsletter* (Supplement), September 1988.

12. Santosh Mehrotra, "The Political Economy of Indo-Soviet Relations," in *Soviet Interests in the Third World*, Robert Cassen, ed. (London: The Royal Institute of International Affairs/ SAGE Publications, 1985), 228.

13. Ivanov, "The Soviet Union in a Changing Global Economic Setting," 17; L. Zevin, "Nekotorye voprosy ekonomicheskogo sotrudnichestva SSSR s razvivayushchimisia stranami" [Some problems of USSR's economic cooperation with the developing countries], *Mirovaya Ekonomika i Mezhdunarodnye Otnosheniya*, no. 3 (March 1988): 41–51. A similar stand, though for different reasons, is taken for Eastern Europe by István Dobozi, *East-South Economic Relations: Patterns, Determinants, and Prospects*, Studies on Developing Countries no. 124 (Budapest: Institute for World Economics of the Hungarian Academy of Sciences, 1988), 22–27.

14. Vyacheslav Seltsovski, "The Structure of the USSR's Foreign Trade and Ways to Improve It," *Foreign Trade, USSR*, no. 11 (1988): 10–13.

15. Bhushan, "Role of Aid and Technology Transfer," 213.

16. Marga Institute of Sri Lanka, "Major Issues Arising from the Transfer of Technology: A Case Study of Sri Lanka" (Geneva: UNCTAD, 1975).

17. Padma Desai, "Transfer of Technology from Centrally Planned and Market Economies to Developing Countries," Paper presented to the second World Congress on Soviet and East European Studies, Garmisch-Partenkirchen, West Germany, 1980.

18. Mehrotra, "The Political Economy of Indo-Soviet Relations," 234.

19. Bhushan, "Role of Aid and Technology Transfer," 224.

20. Graziani, "Influence and Policy Implications of the Major Factors in Inter-Systems Trade."

21. Giovanni Graziani, "Concorrenza tra PVS e Paesi dell'Est sui Mercati del Terzo Mondo" [Competition between developing countries and the East on the Third World markets], Paper presented to the fourth AISSEC meeting, Sorrento, Italy, October 19–20, 1987.

22. Giovanni Graziani, "L'Impact des réformes économiques de l'URSS sur ses échanges avec le Tiers-Monde," in *L'URSS en Transition 1975-1995*, J. Sapir, ed. (Paris: L'Harmattan, forthcoming).

23. Igor Doronin, "Monetary Instruments in External Economic Ties of the USSR: Problems of Their Improvement," Part 2, *Foreign Trade, USSR*, no. 6 (1988): 26.

24. Seltsovski, "The Structure of the USSR's Foreign Trade," 11.

25. Pascal Charpentier and Dominique Meurs, "Les échanges non identifiés dans le commerce de l'U.R.S.S. avec l'Asie du Sud-Ouest," *Revue d'Études Comparatives Est-Ouest* 15, no. 2 (June 1984): 29-46; Pascal Charpentier and Dominique Meurs, *Projection économique de l'URSS en Asie du Sud-Ouest* (Paris: CIRPES, 1985); Déprés, "Les ventes d'armes de l'URSS," 57-73.

26. Moshe Efrat, "The Economics of Soviet Arms Transfers to the Third World," Part 2, in *The Economics of Soviet Arms*, Peter Wiles and Moshe Efrat, eds. (London: Suntory-Toyota International Centre for Economics and Related Disciplines, the London School of Economics and Political Science, 1985).

27. Saadet Deger, "Soviet Arms Sales to Developing Countries: The Economic Forces," in *Soviet Interests in the Third World*, Robert Cassen, ed. (London: The Royal Institute of International Affairs/Sage Publications, 1985), 159-176.

Chapter 5

1. Graziani, "Commercial Relations between Developing Countries and the USSR."

2. *Delovoe sotrudnichestvo v interesakh mira i progressa* [Business cooperation in the interest of peace and progress] (Moscow: Gospolitizdat, 1984), 273.

3. A. L. Belchuk, ed., *SSSR-razvivayushchiesia strany: torgovo-ekonomicheskie otnosheniya* [USSR-developing countries: Commercial and economic relations] (Moscow: Mezhdunarodnye otnosheniya, 1985), 133.

4. Sumitra Chishti, "Experience of India in Trade and Economic Relations with the Socialist Countries of Eastern Europe

and Its Relevance to Developing Countries," UNCTAD TD/B/753, August 17, 1979, p. 8; Suresh Kumar, "Special Trade and Payments Arrangements: Genesis, Development, Problems and Prospects," in *Indo-CMEA Economic Relations*, Suresh Kumar, ed., 85-185.

5. Alan Smith, "Soviet Trade Relations with the Third World," in *Soviet Interests in the Third World*, Robert Cassen, ed., 154.

6. Bartlomiej Kaminski, "External Dimension of Balance of Payments Adjustment in Eastern Europe," in *Osteuropa-Wirtschaft* 33. Jg., 2 (1988), 122-139.

7. Doronin, "Monetary Instruments," 24.

8. *Third World Countertrade* (Newbury, Berkshire, England: Produce Studies, 1988).

9. Michel Kostecki, "Should One Countertrade?" *Journal of World Trade Law* 21, no. 2 (April 1987): 7-21.

Chapter 6

1. Mikhail Khaldin, "Present Forms of USSR Trade and Economic Co-operation with the Developing Countries," *Foreign Trade, USSR*, no. 3 (1984): 24-30; Mikhail Khaldin, "Industrial and Economic Co-operation between the USSR and Developing Countries: Joint Venture Aspects," Paper presented to UNCTAD/UNDP Interregional Workshop, Moscow, December 6-8, 1988.

2. Eugène Zaleski, "Socialist multinationals in developing countries," in *Red Multinationals or Red Herrings: The Activities of Enterprises from Socialist Countries in the West*, Geoffrey Hamilton, ed. (London: Frances Pinter, 1986), 156-184; Carl McMillan, *Multinationals from the Second World: Growth of Foreign Investments by Soviet and East European State Enterprises* (London: Macmillan, 1987).

3. Giovanni Graziani, "Des Multinationales à l'Est?" *Revue d'Économie Industrielle*, no. 28 (2ème trimestre, 1984): 36-58; Graziani, "The Non-European Members of Comecon," 163-179.

4. *IUCCI Newsletter* (Supplement).

5. V. Kononov and Y. Onishchuk, "Soviet Union – Turkey: New Forms of Economic and Technical Co-operation," *Foreign Trade, USSR*, no. 8 (1988): 25.

6. Sibylle Busch, Karl-Hermann Fink, Richard Mikton, and Paul T. Maricle, *Industrial Co-operation between East and West in Third Countries* (Köln: Bundesverband der Deutschen Industrie e.v., 1982), 95.

7. Ibid., 71.

8. Gerard Ballot and Patrick Gutman, "Political Economy of East-West-South Industrial Cooperation," in *East European Economies: Slow Growth in the 1980s*, vol. 2 (Washington, D.C.: U.S. Congress, Joint Economic Committee, March 1986), 115–146.

9. "Tripartite Industrial Co-operation: Current Trends and Prospects," Paper presented at Symposium on East-West Business Opportunities and Trade Prospects, UN ECE TRADE/SEM.8/R.6, Thessaloniki, Greece, September 8–11, 1986, p. 12.

10. Nikolai Kurilovich, "Construction of Projects in Third Countries," *Foreign Trade, USSR*, no. 1 (1988): 30.

11. "Tripartite Industrial Co-operation," 5.

12. Kurilovich, "Construction of Projects in Third Countries," 27.

Index

Afghanistan, 3, 19, 20–21t, 23, 28, 38, 40, 47, 48, 50, 53, 75, 76, 84, 86, 87
Africa. *See specific countries*
Agriculture, 10, 27, 43, 49. *See also* Foodstuffs
Algeria, 20t, 38, 47, 54, 60, 69, 91
Angola, 3, 5, 20t, 37–40, 48, 54, 56, 91
Argentina, 7, 35–40, 47, 49, 50, 61–62, 79, 80, 86, 88–89
Arms sales, x, 68–71; convertible currency surplus and, 73; as export residue, 43–47; oil imports and, 55, 78; raw materials and, 50; Third World indebtedness, 22
Asia. *See specific countries*
Austria, 24

Balance of trade, xi, 72–75; Cuba and, 95; mode of settlement and, 75–80; reciprocal trade vs., 79
Bangladesh, 20t, 50, 61, 75, 76
Barter trade: with India, x; machinery, 61; manufactured goods, 59; military equipment, 70, 78; for oil, 56, 78
Bilateral clearing accounts, 75–79, 96–97
Bolivia, 59, 86
Brazil, 7, 20t, 21, 35, 47, 50, 53, 58, 59, 79, 80–81, 86–88
Brezhnev, Leonid, 4, 6
Bulgaria, 99
Burma, 50
Buyback arrangements, 84–85

Cameroon, 50, 76
Canada, 24
Chad, 76
China, People's Republic of, 2, 5, 57, 58, 80, 87, 89, 99; buyback deals, 85; disarmament and, 3; food exports, 50; minerals exports, 51–52; trade diversification, 48
Class formation, 6
Clearing accounts, 75–79, 96–97
CMEA. *See* Council for Mutual Economic Assistance
Collective farms, 49
Colombia, 61, 63

111

Communist Party of the Soviet Union (CPSU), 2, 4, 5

Competition, with Soviet exports, xi, 65, 96

Congo, 50, 61, 76, 85

Consumer goods, 59, 60, 97

Consumption, development models and, 9

Conversion deals, 57, 85–86

Convertibility, of ruble, 14, 96, 98

Convertible currency. *See* Hard currency

Cooperation. *See* Economic cooperation

Coproduction, 86

Cotton, 57, 85–86

Council for Mutual Economic Assistance (CMEA): bilateral clearing accounts, 76; criticism of, xv, 5; EC and, 2; economic assistance share, x, 18–19; efficiency of aid utilization, 26–28; fuel trade with, 53; GATT and, 98–100; indebtedness of, 22; joint ventures with, 87–89; observer status, 5; price subsidies, 17; Soviet manufactures and, 61; Soviet support of, 95; Soviet trade with, 31–34, 38–40; structure of economic dependence, 53; trade balance with, 75. *See also specific countries*

Countertrade, 56, 80–82, 93–94, 97. *See also* Trade

CPSU. *See* Communist Party of the Soviet Union

Cuba, 5; aid to, 19–21t, 23, 26–28; GATT and, 98; Soviet trade with, 38–40, 48, 50, 51, 80, 95; third markets, 91; trade balance with, 95. *See also* Council for Mutual Economic Assistance

Cyprus, 87

Czechoslovakia, 98

Debt, to Soviet Union, 22–25, 75–80, 89

Deferred compensation, 85

Developing countries: competiton with Soviets, xi, 65; export-import share, 30–34; income analysis, 35; indebtedness of, 22–23; international organizations and, 100; major export categorization, 35; NIEO and, 11–12; North-South structure, 43; socialist-oriented, 5–6; socioeconomic typology of, 7–9; Soviet policy reassessment towards, 3–7. *See also* Trade; *specific countries, problems*

Development models, 9–10, 13–15

Disarmament, 3

Economic assistance: as bilateral, 25; conditions of, 24; criticism of, 5, 26; efficiency of, 26–29; financial terms, 23–24; food aid, 25; geographical distributions, 18–22; industrial projects, 25–26, 61; overall value of, 16–18; quality of, 23–26; restructuring and, 27–28. *See also specific countries*

Economic cooperation: conversion deals, 85–86; coproduction, 86; joint ventures, 86–91; production sharing, 84–85; third markets, 91–92; tripartite industrial cooperation, 92–94; turnkey contracts, 83–84

Economic classes, 7–9

Ecuador, 86

Egypt, 20–23, 38, 47, 50, 57, 73, 76, 88

Elyanov, Anatoly, 8

Equity shares, debt as, 89

Ethiopia, 5, 9, 20t, 23, 25, 28, 38–
40, 48, 53, 86
European Community (EC), 2, 15
Exchange rates, oil imports and,
55
Exports, Soviet: of arms, x, xix,
68–71; competition and, xi,
65, 96; developing countries
share, 30; development
models, 10; of fuels, xviii, 47,
52–56; of machinery, 60–67; of
manufactured goods, 43–47,
60–67; *perestroika* and, 13; re-
exports, 54, 73, 78; residues,
31, 34, 43–47, 68–69, 77;
specialization, 65, 66; structure of, 43–48; technical
quality of, 66–67, 96. *See also*
Trade

Federal Republic of Germany, 17,
24
Financial terms, 23–24
Fisheries, 88
Foodstuffs, 46; buyback deals, 85;
economic assistance of, 25;
joint ventures, 90–91; Soviet
imports of, 43, 48–50
Foreign aid. *See* Economic
assistance
Foreign policy, interdependency
in, 2
Foreign trade. *See* Trade
Foreign trade yearbook, 31, 77
France, 24, 64
Fuels, xviii, 43, 47, 52–56. *See also*
Oil

General Agreement on Tariffs and
Trade (GATT), 2, 15, 98–100
Ghana, 23, 50, 73
Gorbachev, Mikhail, 1, 6–7, 19
Grain, 49, 62
Gross national product (GNP),
economic assistance vs., 16–
18

Guinea, 20t, 28, 51, 61, 73
Guyana, 51, 61

Hard currency: arms sales and,
69–70; debt repayment, 25;
export residue and, 77; joint
ventures and, 14; oil imports
and, 54; Soviet trade balance
and, xvii, 72; tripartite
industrial cooperation and,
94
High-technology industry, 10,
41
Hong Kong, 35–37, 66, 86
Hungary, 98

IMF. *See* International Monetary
Fund
Imports, Soviet: consumer goods,
59, 97; developing countries
share, xvii–xviii, 30; of food,
43, 48–50; of fuels, xviii, 47,
52–56; of machinery, 57–58; of
manufactured goods, xviii–
xix, 56–61; from NICs, 35–37;
nontariff restrictions on, 98;
of raw materials, 50–52;
reported vs. actual, 31, 34;
structure of, 43, 44t. *See also*
Trade
Income, national socioeconomic
class and, 8, 35
India: bilateral clearing accounts,
76; buyback deals, 84–85;
clearing agreement with, 96–
97; coproduction, 86; countertrade with, 80–81; criticism
of Soviets, 78; economic
assistance share, 18–21;
Gorbachev and, 6–7, 19;
interest rates and, 23–24; joint
ventures, 87, 90; Soviet
machinery and, 62–64; Soviet
trade with, 38–40, 47–48, 50–
53, 57–58, 62–64, 73–75;
special export zones, 58;

India (*continued*)
    structural surplus, 77
Indonesia, 7, 41, 50
Industry: development models
    and, 10; raw material imports
    and, 51; Soviet concentration
    in, 25–26; Soviet equipment
    and, 62–65; tripartite industri-
    al cooperation, 92–94
Infrastructure development, 26
Interest rates, 23–24
International Monetary Fund
    (IMF), 2, 15, 24, 98
International organizations, 2, 15,
    98–100
Iran, 7, 10, 53–54, 56, 61, 76, 87,
    91
Iraq, 38, 47, 54, 56, 69, 73, 80
Italy, 64
Ivanov, Ivan, 1
Ivory Coast, 50, 73

Jamaica, 51, 61
Japan, 2, 17, 24, 64
Joint ventures, 4, 14, 86–91

Kampuchea, 3, 10, 18, 20–21t, 76,
    85
Khrushchev, Nikita, 6, 9
Kuwait, 56, 87

Laos, 5, 18–21t, 76, 85
Latin America. *See specific
    countries*
Least-developed countries (LDCs),
    8, 23
Libya, 38–40, 47, 91; arms sales
    to, 3, 69; trade balance with,
    73
Loans, financial terms, 23–24. *See
    also* Economic assistance

Machinery, 57–58, 77
Madagascar, 20t, 22, 23, 85
Malaysia, 7, 42, 50

Manufactured goods: coproduction,
    86; countertrade and, 81, 97;
    Soviet exports of, 43–47, 60–
    67; Soviet imports of, xviii–
    xix, 37, 43, 56–61; technical
    standards and, 66–67
Mexico, 7, 58, 60, 61, 86
Middle East. *See specific countries*
Minerals, 50–52, 84–85
Ministry of Foreign Economic
    Relations, 13
Mongolia, 19–23, 26–28, 48, 51–
    52, 61, 85. *See also* Council for
    Mutual Economic Assistance
Morocco, 50, 53, 84, 88, 91
Most-favored nation status, 99
Mozambique, 5, 20t, 23, 25, 89

Natural gas, 53–54
Nepal, 75, 76
Netherlands, 24
New Economic Policy (NEP), 10
New International Economic
    Order (NIEO), 11–12
Newly industrializing countries
    (NICs): GATT and, 100;
    Soviet trade with, xvi, 35, 40–
    41, 48; third market deals, 91–
    92; trade balances, 77. *See
    also specific countries*
Nicaragua, 5, 19, 20t, 25, 28, 38–
    40, 53
Nigeria, 23, 61, 88, 89, 91
Nontariff restrictions, 98
North Korea, 5, 18–21t, 51, 48, 57,
    58, 85–88

Official development assistance
    (ODA), 17
Oil, 52–56; arms barter deals and,
    70, 78; buyback deals, 84; re-
    export of, 54, 73, 78; trade
    balance and, 73
Oil imbroglio, xviii, 53
Oman, 7, 56

Organization of Petroleum
    Exporting Countries (OPEC),
    24, 55–56, 77

Pakistan, 57, 76, 86
Panama, 86, 90
Perestroika, ix–x, 13–15
Peru, 22, 23, 50, 57, 58
Petroleum. *See* Oil
Philippines, 7
Poland, 98
Price structure, 14, 98
Price subsidies, 17
Production-sharing, 84–85
Profitability, currency convertibil-
    ity and, 14, 96
Protectionism, joint ventures vs.,
    89

Quality, Soviet exports, 66–67, 96

Raw materials: buyback deals, 84–
    85; countertrade, 81; imports
    of, 50–52; price subsidies, 17
Redeployment, of production
    lines, 59
Re-export, of oil, 54, 73, 78
Repayment, Third World debt;
    goods as, 24, 60; in hard
    currency, 25; mode of settle-
    ment, 75–80
Residue, of exports, 31, 34, 43–47,
    68–69, 77
Romania, 98
Ruble, convertibility of, 14, 96, 98

Saudi Arabia, 7, 49, 54, 73
Scholarships, 17
Senegal, 76
Service industry, 97
Sheinis, Victor, 8
Shevardnadze, Eduard, 7
Singapore, 35, 37, 53, 58, 66, 87
Socialist countries, trade with, 18,
    31–34. *See also* Council for

Mutual Economic Assistance
    (CMEA); *specific countries*
Socialist-oriented developing
    countries, 5–6, 9, 95. *See also*
    specific countries
South Korea, 2, 7, 9, 35, 40–41, 66
South Yemen, 5, 20t, 23, 25, 38–
    40, 54, 56, 61, 76
Sovfintrade organization, 81
Soviet Far East, 41
Soviet Union. *See* Trade; *specific*
    activities, problems
Special economic zones, 41
Sri Lanka, 20t, 63
Sudan, 73, 76
Syria, 20t, 23, 38, 47, 48, 54, 56,
    57, 69, 76, 84

Taiwan, 7, 9, 35, 40–41, 66
Tanzania, 20t, 76
Technical assistance, 61–64, 84, 92
Textiles, 57, 85–86
Thailand, 7, 50, 59, 87
Third markets, 91–92
Third World. *See* Developing
    countries
Trade: analysis by economic
    criteria, 34–37; commodity
    composition of, 43–48;
    conversion deals, 57; coun-
    tertrade, 80–82; distribution
    of, 32–33t, 36t, 37–40; GDP
    vs., 35; mixed payment mode,
    76; modes of settlements, 75–
    80; new directions of, 40–42;
    New International Economic
    Order, 11–12; North-South
    structure, 43; obstacles to, 96;
    price subsidies, 17; production
    redeployment, 59; residues,
    43–47; systems analysis of,
    31–34. *See also* Balance of
    trade; Exports, Soviet;
    Imports, Soviet; *specific*
    countries

Tripartite industrial cooperation, 92–94
Tunisia, 61, 76
Turkey, 38–40, 48, 53, 58, 60, 85, 90–92
Turnkey contracts, 83–84

Uganda, 10, 76
United Arab Emirates (UAE), 7, 56, 87, 88
United Nations, Conference on Trade and Development (UNCTAD), 11–12
United Power Corporation, 92
United States, 17, 24

Uruguay, 7, 59, 61

Vanguard parties, 6
Venezuela, 87
Vietnam, 5, 19–23, 26–28, 38–40, 48, 50, 57, 61, 85–86. *See also* Council for Mutual Economic Assistance

World Bank, 15, 98

Yugoslavia, 5, 38–40, 48, 54, 76, 90, 91

Zambia, 22, 23, 51